THE FIGHTING IRISH

To
my
children

May the only arms
they ever know
Be the
arms of love

THE FIGHTING IRISH

by

SEAN McCANN

LESLIE FREWIN of LONDON

Also by Sean McCann

The World of Brendan Behan
The World of Sean O'Casey

The Wit of Brendan Behan
The Wit of the Irish
The Wit of Oscar Wilde
The Wit of Love

The Story of the Abbey Theatre
The Four Square Guide to Ireland

First published in 1972 by
Leslie Frewin Publishers Limited,
Five Goodwin's Court, Saint Martin's Lane,
London WC2N 4LL

This book is set in Bembo,
printed and bound in Great Britain by R. J. Acford Ltd.,
Industrial Estate, Chichester, Sussex

ISBN 85632 007 2

Contents

List of Illustrations

Introduction

THE WORLD HAS long ago come to accept that the Irish love, live, talk and fight with more gusto than any other race. The Irishman will even publicly boast of the monopoly his race has held in matters of wit and literature, generals, admirals, corporals and soldiers, heavyweight champions, satisfied wives and big families. Modesty has never been a characteristic trait of the Irishman. It is only when a man sits down to sift the evidence that he finds the flaws. It isn't easy to prove conclusively that the Irish have been the world's greatest lovers, or the greatest wits, but in the realm of blood, guts and haughty defiance of oppression, persecution, and even the law itself, the Irishman has left enough evidence for the historian of the future to justify Robert E Lee's comment, 'Never were men so brave'.

Quick-tempered and yet still a brooder on hidden angers, he has never been short of a fight, right or wrong, through any stage of history. There were tribal fights, shillelagh fights, battles against the English, amateur and professional fisticuffs, wars in Russia, in America, in Sweden, in France, in Spain, in South Africa, wild Colonial mêlées and always battles against . . . the English. Every man in the world could be his enemy or his friend but the English as a race allowed themselves the singular honour of being sorted out as the most reliable of enemies. An eighteenth-century Irish toast ran:

A wet winter to you
A dry Spring
A bloody Summer
And no King.

But the English have generally proved elusive enemies and so the Irishman has had to purge his frustrations in other wars in other places. Finley Peter Dunne, the Irish-American humourist, put the Irishman's real feelings into words when he said: 'You can refuse to love a man or to lend him money, but if he wants to fight you have got to oblige him.'

The obligation to fight is there for ever in Irish life. The names of Derry, Clontarf, Aughrim, Boyne, Eureka, and now Derry again burn a deep scar on the history of the Irish as fighters, scar so deep that the hurt will be there almost as long as the mark.

The heritage of fifty years of brooding erupted in 1969 to pitch the Irish into the world's eyes once again, and the continued, absolute inability of the English to cope – they have been trying for eight centuries – with the Irish question was more evident than ever. Chesterton could never have foreseen the bitter fangs gnashing with such venom when he wrote that the 'great Gaels of Ireland are the men that God made mad, for all their wars are happy and all their songs are sad'.

1969 was just another chapter in the story of a race that is always said to be spoiling for a fight, but this time it wasn't one of the happy wars, religious wars never are, and a deep chasm of religious strife cuts through the history of Ireland from Derry in 1969 right back hundreds and hundreds of years. Long before he would fight for himself the Irishman has fought for his religion. And these fights of his have been no devil-may-care adventures but bitter, disastrous forays that still rankle. And if religion didn't rear its head, what better to fight for than adventure, generally in the guise of money? When word got out that in England the gentlemen were paying huge purses to bare-knuckle boxers as a sporting spectacle, the Irish invasion began and soon the ranks of English champions were led by Irishmen. The mercenary streak in the Irish make-up is nothing new: they had gone before to fight in cold Crimea; sunburnt Egypt; travelled with and against the Cherokee, the Chicksaw, the Muskogee; helped Napoleon against Wellington and Wellington against Napoleon; the Confederates against the Union and the English against just about every invader and opponent that fought against the Georges, Edwards, Henrys and Elizabeths. It might have been paradise to fight against the English but, damn it, weren't you paid to fight for them?

But some might say even more mercenary, surely, is the fact that in war after war the Irish appeared on both sides, making sure that right was with them one way or the other. When the warring Clare's Dragoons heaped fire and brimstone on the English on Ramillies' bloody field no doubt there were many of their own race, even other Claremen, there in the defeated ranks. In the American Civil War it is said that 150,000 Irishmen fell and an equal number returned to civilian life, and they were just about equally divided between the North and South. Even in England's homemade wars the Irish were there on the side of the red rose or the white, and when faced with this 'dishonesty of principle' would only reply that, no matter what side you were on, you were sure of having the satisfaction of having Englishmen against you.

To find the complete image makers of the fighting Irishman means one has to inhabit the pages of fact, legend and lore before coming eye to eye with the battlers who established the tradition. In full battle array the soldiers of chivalry, the chief fighting men, the avengers of insults, even the doormen seem to be much more than a common breed. The nine doormen of King Conari the Great in the first century stood 'threateningly' at the door of the palace and allowed no one to enter who did not give a satisfactory account of himself. Imagine with doormen painted so fiercely what the cut of a champion must have been. Pick one; let it be

Triscatal. He was 'mighty, broadfronted, shaggy-haired with thighs as thick as an ordinary man's body, wearing a thick leathern apron from his armpits down, his limbs were bare and his aspect was so fierce that he killed men by his very look'.

He was very much the gladiator of his tribe or province and it was usual for him to throw down a challenge to single combat by standing in front of a hostile camp or fort and thumping on his shield. This arrogance prompted the Irish to coin a phrase for a swaggering bully that is still part of the language – even today the fellow looking for a fight is called a 'boolim-skee' (in Irish *Baulim-sciath*, which literally means 'I strike (or hit) the shield'). But the real champion was a lot more than just a bully and when he had well proved his worth he was decorated with the champion's collar and called *nia-naisc* ('champion of the collar'), an honour very similar to the British Knight of the Garter.

The tradition of battle was great and one writer has said that the greatest investment any Irishman can make is in a good enemy. Certainly this was true in old Ireland and no man of any importance was without his own private army. There were military colleges, too, all set to train the leaders – King Cormac Mac Art founded three of them, one in military science. Pity then the man who believes that all fighting was with a heavy shillelagh, brute force and ignorance. Every chieftain's son was expected to go through a full course of military training – and even long before this he would get a taste of what was to come when his mother presented the first piece of solid food to him on the point of a sword. An old ballad of 1780 put the action into words:

The infants at the breast could practise every motion
And had of a battle an excellent notion
Even mountainy rustics who never ate bread
Could fire without blinking or bobbing their head.

In this tradition the most glorious battle group in ancient Ireland was born – the Red Branch Knights. Here boys were often brought into the service at seven years of age. There were times when the requirements were less fixed but still tough. Then entry into knighthood was suspended until a boy was able to fight, and in Ulster the custom really had a blood-curdling condition. The candidate for knighthood who took arms had to enter the province of Connacht 'on a foray and there to slay a human being'. No wonder Cromwell later equated Connacht with hell. When they were fully-fledged knights they lived up to this honour, as Richard II found out when he visited Ireland in 1494. He suggested that he should confer knighthoods on four provincial kings – O'Connor, O'Neill, MacMurrough and O'Brien. But they told him they didn't need it – they were well knighted already in a tradition older than the English!

Knights though they were, not even the very chivalrous Red Branch Knights were above the superstitions of war, a trait that has remained in the Irish race to this very day. Their greatest warring superstition was that a sling shot made from the brains of a defeated warrior was the most dangerous weapon of all. 'It was the custom of the Ulstermen', goes one description, 'that from every champion they killed in single combat to take the brains out of their heads and mix lime with them until they formed a hard ball.' Easy as it might seem to brush this gory suggestion aside as a tall tale there is evidence that such odd composition balls did exist – one of them can still be seen in Dublin's National Museum.

After the Red Branch came the Fianna, the real élite of ancient battlers. They lasted on the Irish scene for just about a century but eventually were bedevilled by the old Irish trait 'Holier than thou' and suffered the consequences. They were something of a fly-by-night band who, like the mercenaries, tended to change their loyalties according to the whims of their leaders. This was their undoing for they set up a military junta to rule the country but in swift retribution the ruling king of the time set out and annihilated them in the battle of Gavra, near Skreen in County Meath.

Before they went they had set up one of the most efficient fighting forces the land had ever known. Their leader Finn – whether legendary or not – has been looked upon down the years as a great general. Even the Scottish historian, Pinkerton, who said few nice things about the Irish, had to agree that here was a case that deserved every commendation. Writing about Finn and the Fianna, he said:

> He seems to have been a man of great talents for the age, and of celebrity in arms. His formation of a regular standing army, trained to war, in which all the Irish accounts agree, seems to have been a rude imitation of the Roman legions in Britain. The idea, though simple enough, shows prudence for such a force alone could have coped with the Romans had they invaded Ireland.

Through the annals of Irish history runs this great streak of personalities – men who lived just for war. Not only was there Finn but also Cuchulainn, a mythical character, who could fight and beat the greatest, and whose deeds are all part of the great hero legend associated with the Red Branch Knights. It is hard indeed to sort the history out from the legend as many of the great Irishmen of even recent years – Wolfe Tone, Daniel O'Connell, Patrick Pearse – could so easily have been figments of the imagination, and few fiction sagas could rival the fantastic doings and wanderings of the O'Neill and O'Donnell families. The traditions for fighting and warring are all there and have been ever since the Irish set up a running invasion of England that lasted almost four centuries. They crossed battleaxes against the Picts, the Romans and the Britons. It is claimed that it was the Roman general, Theodosius, who put a stop to the invading Irish, but only for a time until Niall of the Nine Hostages set off to plunder again. The Roman poet Claudian found that 'the ocean foamed with their hostile oars'. Niall even took himself to Gaul but his ambition and the Irish tendency to battle among themselves was his undoing and he was assassinated by one of his own chiefs on the banks of the Loire. This was really a turning point, for the next invader out of Ireland, Niall's successor Dathi, was killed in AD 428 by a flash of lightning at the foot of the Alps, soon after his followers had destroyed a hermitage. Superstitions being very much a part of their make-up, the Irish interpreted this as a divine message and took themselves home.

So you can go through the history of the land picking from these ancient tales and legends the stories of some of the most fantastic heroes to illustrate anyone's ancestry. One old story that has been handed down in my own family was of a distant ancestor who used to have his own litany: 'St Patrick by your word guide me; Cuchulainn by your strength protect me, Finn by your learning teach me and Cearnach by your virtuosity may I beat the head off him.' Well we know of St Patrick, Finn and Cuchulainn but this Cearnach who achieved such lasting fame does, in a macabre way, deserve it. He was Conall Cearnach, one of the greatest enemies of Connacht, and he coudn't go to sleep at night without crushing the head of a Connacht man under his knee. No doubt he had to practise virtuosity to catch a man from Connacht every day of the week!

These then were the forerunners of the men who fought in just about every major battle in the five continents in the past six centuries. They had been reared on war and any man who couldn't or wouldn't fight could find little comfort in Ireland. Unfortunately the time was soon to come when not even the men who could fight were able to find a resting place here. This was the cruellest blow and it sent out in the first years of the seventeenth century the great hordes of men who wandered the world so widely that they are to this day known as the Wild Geese. In Irish history it is called the Flight of the Earls, when the O'Neills and the O'Donnells, the great hopes of Ireland, were followed into exile by boat-loads of common soldiers who had left following defeat by the English at Kinsale in 1601. These were the descendants of Cuchulainn, Finn and Cearnach and the ancestors of the Fighting 69th, the Irish Brigade of France, the Irish Musketeers of Austria, the Inniskilling Dragoons of the Somme, . . . the ancestors of the unruly ones like Ned Kelly, Billy the Kid . . . of heroes like Davy Crockett, Stonewall Jackson, Montgomery of Alamein . . . and of a tradition carried on through Russia, India, Eureka, Bull Run, Fontenoy, North Africa . . . anywhere indeed where there was even the chance of a fight.

PART I

The World's A Big Place

CHAPTER I

The Wild Geese

THERE IS ONE thing you can say about the Irish: they have spent more time putting the fear of God into man than any other race on earth. If they couldn't do it according to the Bible, they did it according to the sword. There may not have been many of them at times, but they created more noise than any other nation. One of the earliest to acknowledge this was Louis XIV when he complained to one of the officers of the Irish Brigade that the Irish caused him more trouble than the rest of his army put together. Only an Irishman could have provided the apt reply to this one. 'Please, Your Majesty,' replied the officer, 'your enemies make the same complaint about them.'

Louis ought to have known better than to make such a remark about the Irish Brigade, for no other foreigner has left such an impression on the land of France before or since, than the Wild Geese who landed there in flocks right through the seventeenth and eighteenth centuries. Their loyalty was never in doubt, neither was their courage. They set their own standards when the Regiment of Mountcashel, the fragmentary remains of a regiment defeated at Enniskillen in Ireland, went into their first mobilised battle on French soil. Along with other corps of the Irish Brigade, they had their baptism of fire in the victorious army of Marshal de Catinat in Piedmont. It was in August 1690, a time when the fighting was at its greatest, that the Mountcashel Regiment went into operation; the fury of their attack carried all before it. The defeated Victor Amadeus realised that it was the Irish who had beaten him: '*Ma foi*, what soldiers!' he said. 'If I only had a thousand such, not only Piedmont, but the whole of France would be mine tomorrow.' He wasn't alone in his praise; the evening after the battle, Catinat took himself to the Irish quarters and warmly congratulated them.

This was the standard that the whole Irish Brigade set throughout some three centuries in the service of France; always first into the fray they earned more laurels than any other similar contingent. Credit should be given to the French for realising the value of the Irish as fighters. They did everything they could to welcome the men who had been beaten out of their own country, first by war, then by the most heinous laws of Cromwell and Elizabeth. After one battle, one of the Austrian generals turned to an Irish officer who had chosen the Austrian service and said: 'The French are no longer men – they're devils.'

'True,' replied the Irishman, 'it is because of my own countrymen. Louis, knowing there are no fighters in the world like the Irish, has lured them into his service. It is they who are responsible for all these wild rushes; the French are trying to keep up with them.'

The English too – at least some of them – felt badly about the loss of the Irish. Marlborough frequently found that it was the Irish Brigade that was responsible for the abject failure of his missions: 'There is no counting on anything when these Irish firebrands are about,' he complained, 'they appear when least expected, do what is least expected and render tactics, strategies and generals equally hopeless and abortive. There is one thing to be thankful for, however, their recruiting ground is a long way off.' Regardless of how far off the recruiting ground was, the

Irish Brigade was able to maintain its strength on French soil for a long time.

The first three regiments of infantry to form the Brigade were the Mountcashel, the O'Briens and the Dillon, commanded respectively by Lord Mountcashel (Justin MacCarthy), Colonel Daniel O'Brien and Colonel the Honourable Arthur Dillon. They established the first footing on French soil but they were soon followed in 1691 by some twenty thousand others who arrived in Brest after the defeat of King James's army at Limerick. They travelled in a collection of ships that ranged from a Galway hooker to a fully rigged man-o'-war. This great exodus, the first of many, brought together thousands of men nursing a common grievance; nothing was more natural than that they should band together. Altogether they formed two troops of Horse Guards, two troops of horse, two of dragoons that were to serve as infantry, eight regiments of foot and three independent companies. Eventually some thirty thousand men from Ireland marched under the flag of France.

But wherever they went they never forgot Ireland, and the almost indifferent way they treated war lent full justification to the comment that 'they make merry soldiers'. So strong indeed was their love of things Irish that they refused to march to French martial tunes. The French agreed to let them use their own although they had previously refused a similar request from a Swiss regiment. Possibly they realised that the chances of the Irish ever getting home were slight and that they were entitled to some moments of nostalgia.

Practically all the soldiers in the early Brigade were veterans of the great war that two foreign kings – James and William – fought on Irish soil, a war that is still well remembered. Drogheda and Limerick still hold a bold place in Irish history but the one stark name that will never be wiped out is the Boyne. From this one encounter stems the Orange and Green conflict that, even today, rips Ireland in two. The Williamite Orangemen won and have never let the world forget it – this is not to say that if the forces of James had been victorious they wouldn't have provided a memory just as long and as bitter for their supporters. But what is certain is that if the forces of James had won, there would not have been the great exodus of soldiers from Ireland at the end of the seventeenth century. Certainly they remembered the Boyne and when facing the English in war their wild battle cry often was, 'Remember the Boyne.' But before they really got a chance to have a crack at the English, the Brigade fought some of the bloodiest battles in the Italian and German campaigns and though their reputation was enhanced, it was at a terrible cost.

'The Irish Brigade grows thinner every day,' reflected one Irish officer; 'pray to God that the holding of the last wake does not fall to me.' And another spoke sadly after the battle of Kempten: 'The number of our widows grows faster than the shamrock round Kenmare; pray to Heaven that a few of us will be left to tell them how we died; how we thought of them – and of Ireland.'

There was little need to tell people: already the French nation knew well how much it owed to the Irish, and Louis showed his appreciation with frequent decorations. But decorations themselves were not enough; the lifeblood of the Brigade was an infusion of new soldiers to the three main regiments. These were provided first by active recruitment in Ireland, illegally and at some risk, and secondly by the amalgamation of some of the smaller regiments and companies that marched under their own flags. The list of these regiments is a long one. Apart from the Mountcashel, O'Brien and Dillon Regiments, there were the Corps of Horse Guards; Royal Irish Regiment; King and Queen's

Regiment of Horse; King's Regiment of Dismounted Dragoons; Colonel Walter Bourke's Regiment of Foot (also known as the Athlone); the King's Royal Regiment of Foot Guards; the Queen's Regiment of Infantry; the Infantry Regiment of the Marine (the greatest name changers in the Brigade – they changed titles with most new commanders and were the Albemarle, Fitzgerald and O'Donnell). Then under the smaller group of companies there were the Dublin, Limerick, Athlone, Galway, Cloncarty, Bourke, Sheldon, Berwick and other companies.

So when it was time to face the old reliable once again, the Irish Brigade was back to its original strength. The battle was Dettigen in 1743, and although the praise for the Irish was great, the soldiers of George II won another fine battle. Two years later came Fontenoy, and there were 3,870 soldiers standing first in line. Frequently, over the years, there have been doubts expressed about the part the Irish played in this battle, which was probably England's greatest military disaster of the century. The traditional Irish view is that a wild, daring charge at a very crucial moment won the battle for France; on the other hand, some historians have called this interpretation no more than a fanciful legend. Others haven't expressed any opinion and mentioned the Irish Brigade as just being part of the French forces.

The battle took place on 11th May 1745, and was one of the many engagements in the War of Austrian Succession which had begun five years earlier. During that time it had been brought right up to the French borders, so, in an effort to open up the Austrian Netherlands, the French laid siege to the town of Tournai. When an Allied army, some 65,000 strong, marched to relieve Tournai the French took up positions on a plateau five miles to the south-west of the besieged town. The French army, led by Marshal Maurice de Saxe, knew every move of the Allied army led by the Duke of Cumberland, who seems to have had a pretty poor intelligence network operating for him. In the centre of the French line was the village of Fontenoy, on the left the village of Antoing overlooking the River Scheldt, ahead and to the left was the wood of Barry. In and around these, strong fortifications were set up and all was strengthened by a number of redoubts. Marshal de Saxe knew his strength and he settled his soldiers in a rectangular position so that they would not have to face a hostile charge in line – a battle tactic that had proved them wanting in earlier affairs. Among the French reserves were six regiments of the Irish Brigade.

The battle began soon after dawn when the Allies made their first attempt to capture Barry wood. Five hours later the Allied position had not changed one whit and Cumberland was faced with beating a hasty retreat or carrying out a frontal attack on the French. He decided on a frontal attack and in the next two hours one of the most memorable charges ever made by a British army was witnessed beside the hamlet of Fontenoy. Raked continuously by deadly fire from all sides the Allies battled on, advancing over the bodies of their own dead and wounded . . . at last they stood in the centre of the battlefield to all intents and purposes the victors. Up till now the Irish had not been called upon to fight, although the Dillon Regiment, in company with the Normandie and Royal Vaisseaux, had made one unsuccessful and weakening attack. The battle had now reached the point where everything depended on the side that showed the greatest initiative. The man who reacted first was de Saxe. He grouped all his forces and the Irish found themselves on the right, together with the brigade of Normandie and the Royal Vaisseaux. The Irish were first into the fight and tornado-like they charged with a combined roar of 'Remember the Boyne'. This time they got their reward: the English retreated before the madness of the rush, then broke and fled. The Boyne had been avenged to a small extent. The only English colour captured in the whole battle was by Sergeant Wheelock of the Bulkeley section of the Irish Brigade – an act of bravery that was rewarded by his promotion on the field of battle to Second Lieutenant. But it was a battle that cost heavily – seven thousand died on the English side; five thousand on the French, including fifty-three officers, six of them generals. The Irish payment for their astounding impetuosity was heaviest of all individual regiments in the battle – hundreds of men died, including their commander, Colonel James Dillon.

When the battle was over Louis gave testimony to the fact that the Irish breakthrough was the turning point when he rode to the Irish lines and told the troops he owed the victory to them. One Irish officer, his face covered in blood and flanked by two other officers – one with leg wounds and the other unable to see – thanked Louis but remarked: 'Your Majesty, your blessings are like those in the Gospel, they fall upon the lame and the blind.' To add further to his words the king soon after awarded many promotions and gratuities as well as lavishly distributing crosses of St Louis to the Brigade. De Saxe, too, put in his word for the Irish when he wrote: 'The Irish Brigade which was up front behaved as bravely as possible.' George II could well exclaim: 'Sad indeed are the laws that deprive me of such soldiers.' The leading English authority on the battle, Francis Henry Skrine, has applauded the Brigade: 'Among French Infantry Regiments,' he wrote in his *Fontenoy and the War of Austrian Succession*, 'those of the Irish Brigade stood first. Their desperate valour was a factor of great importance in our disaster.'

This 'desperate valour' was something that was never lacking in the soldier of the Irish Brigade. One story tells how in Flanders just as the French front line began to waver and Villeroi, who had vainly tried to rally his men, had almost given up hope, a young officer of the O'Brien Regiment passed by. 'Come here,' shouted the French general. 'See if you can infuse some of your Irish courage into these faint-hearted countrymen of mine.'

'I will, sir,' replied the Irishman – and tearing off his sword belt threw it into the advancing enemy. 'Now to retrieve it,' he roared and threw himself into the fray in front of the French. They followed, and what had looked like almost certain defeat became instead a victory. Villeroi was delighted and sent one of his officers to find the Irishman; but the news came back that he was dead.

'Dead,' moaned the Frenchman, 'a great pity . . . had he lived he would have one day become a marshal.'

It would be nice to think that the story had a happy ending but it is hardly likely, although one authority insists that Villeroi's prediction did come true: the Irishman was only wounded and ten years later he was wearing the uniform of a *Maréchal-de-Camp*.

The Irish Brigade is said to have loved bright colours and smart uniforms. Once when a Frenchman was claiming for his country the invention of all the elegances, he claimed the ruffle; but the Irishman did not despair. 'You may have invented the ruffle,' came the answer, 'but we improved on it – we put it on a shirt.'

There were occasions when history gives the Brigade the greatest credit – for leaving their uniforms behind them. Cremona, besieged by Prince Eugene and defended by the French, was surprised one morning before dawn and might well have been lost but for the promptness of the Irish. While the French were buttoning their tunics and smartening up their ruffles the Irish, at the sound of the trumpet, jumped out of bed and simply buckled on their crossbelts and cartouch boxes, grabbed their guns and raced to the barrack square. As Samuel Lover says about this escapade:

> Their indifference to appearances on this occasion was all the greater that the period was mid-winter and the city was near the Alps. In this condition they were charged by the Austrian Cuirassiers. It was steel coats against nightshirts; but the linen trade of Ireland proved the more formidable of the two. The Austrians were driven back and the French had time to form and recover the town.'

For this the Irish were given a pay increase.

Once again the strength of the Brigade was weakening fast – there was a period of comparative calm in Ireland and recruits were not arriving as fast as they were needed. In 1792 the Brigade was disbanded – fortunately for the men themselves. Had they remained, their fate might have been like that of the massacred Swiss Brigade who stayed on and suffered the price of loyalty in the French Revolution.

But it has always proved hard to keep the Irish away from a fight and about 1800 a new brigade was formed from the survivors, assisted by many United Irishmen who had settled in the country. Again courage was their greatest quality and in the French campaigns in Algiers Irish officers and men were often commended for their bravery. In 1844, when the Arabs were completely routed by the French, the finest soldiers in Morocco were pursued for miles by French cavalry – led, almost inevitably – by an Irishman. But the men in this campaign showed something more than courage. The following year the French had captured a tribe of Arabs in a cave and it was decided to block up the entrance with fires and suffocate all inside, but insistent demands by the Irish to the French general stopped the slaughter.

Somehow, this second brigade never achieved quite the reputation of their predecessors, but still France proved the great neighbour and practically every great Irish fighter since then has gone there: Wolfe Tone, Robert Emmet, Miles Byrne, William

Putnam McCabe, and in later years Maud Gonne and Casement.

Nevertheless, through the eighteenth and nineteenth centuries the Irish Brigade stood by France and fought some of the bloodiest battles: the end came at the close of the Franco-Prussian campaign of 1870. The Irish Brigade went into the final battle of that war with a mere fifty-five men; they came out of it with twenty. At one stage the French general saw their small, ragged and bloody group shortly after they had beaten off a large troop of Uhlans.

'What regiment are you?' he demanded.

'*La Compagnie Irlandaise, Régiment Étranger, mon général,*' came the reply.

'Then,' said the general, 'I would rather have la Compagnie Irlandaise than a battalion of Mobiles.'

To this small tattered remnant fell the distinction of firing the last shots at the Germans. They were actually crossing bayonets with the enemy when a messenger rode up shouting '*Cessez le feu.*'

To this score of men fell the honour of bowing out from the fighting life of France; but they didn't go unremembered. One French paper, *La Franche Comte*, published this tribute to them and to all the Irish Brigade:

> Amongst the volunteers who have come from all parts of Europe to place their swords at the service of France when she was invaded and her independence threatened, we cannot forget the Irish Company, which formed part of the Army of the East. Officers and soldiers, sons of green Erin, they remembered in the hour of our danger the ties of strong sympathy which have for a long time united France and Ireland. Having been the first to come to us, they are the last to leave us, after having borne a brilliant part in the different combats of the East. At Montbeliard they were

> last to leave the field of battle. At Busy they were complimented by General Rebillard. In the name of our poor France thanks, once more thanks, to our Irish brothers; we shall take care faithfully to remember their courage and their devotion.

There can be little doubt that the French editor was speaking for the people at this time and it would be nice to record that at all stages of French history the people of the adopted land felt the same for the Irish soldiers who fought so valiantly for them. Now and again the Irish asked the French the great favour of helping them rid Ireland of the English. They talked but that was all. The French forgot easily and the lives of many great Irishmen finished on the red stained guillotine of France. When the act was done and the life taken the French expressed sorrow and Pontius-like washed their hands of the crime. Certainly this was the case with General the Count de Lally, one of the greatest Irish friends of France. General of the troops of Louis XV in India he showed amazing youthful courage, but his luck turned and after early successes he was forced to surrender under severe handicaps at Pondicherry. The French accused him of selling the war and he was guillotined under the crudest circumstances. Lally wasn't alone in this humiliation: Marshal Arthur Dillon, commander of the once great regiment of Dillon (by this time known as the 87th Regiment of the Line), Governor of Tobago and a Deputy of France was sentenced to death in 1794 a few months after General James O'Moran, commander of French Flanders, had died on the guillotine. When the acts were done France showed her sorrow. She acknowledged then the greatness of those men and the Brigade and the fact that in one century alone 450,000 Irishmen had died in the ranks of France. There could be no doubt that the banner presented to the Regiment in 1792 was justified – it showed the shamrock and the fleur-de-lis interwoven.

CHAPTER 2

After the Flight

IT IS EASY enough to say that in every land brave men find a home – but only a list of the Irishmen who became generals, governors, counts, marshals in the armies of Europe could add credence to it. Not only were the Dillons, Lallys, O'Briens and MacCarthys aided and abetted by just about every other pedigree of the Gael on the side of France, other lands also reaped the benefit. England had a share of Irishmen in her forces – both naval and military – so had Austria, Portugal, Sweden and Russia. At home, Ireland was regarded as a job grabber's delight – by the English nobility – and many a family of gentry would never have been landed had the fertile land across the Irish Sea not been so denuded of its own race, a great number of these dispossessed Irishmen finding their way to Spain.

Spain became the land of the 'O'. O'Neill, O'Donnell, O'Higgins, O'Moore, O'Farrel, O'Daly, O'Donoughue, O'Sullivan found that somehow the Irish temperament was more in accord with the Spanish than with any other on the continent. Like the men who began France's Irish Brigade, the Irish landed in Spain in 1602 soon after the disastrous battle of Kinsale which caused the great Flight of the Earls. Red Hugh O'Donnell was the first of this great gathering to land in Spain in the hope of persuading Philip III to send an expedition to Ulster. When

Red Hugh left Ireland it was recorded that his emigration was greeted with a mournful 'loud clapping of hands, tearful mourning and loud lamentation'. And, according to the scribe, 'they had reason for this at the time for never afterwards did they behold as ruler over them him who was their leader and earthly prince in the land of Erin'.

Red Hugh's voyage ended in bitter disappointment; Philip, like most European monarchs of the time, was too busy with his own wars and had little time for the Irishman. This set the pattern of the Irish chief's visit and less than nine months after arriving in Spain he was 'attacked with a violent sickness and died,' poisoned, it is said, by a spy of Elizabeth I. Other O'Donnells followed and for hundreds of years right through to the Spanish Civil War the Irish were there on Spanish soil fighting on one side or another and generally there was an O'Donnell in high command.

This clan from the north-eastern corner of Ireland certainly played a great part in the European wars of three centuries. Apart from those who fought in Spain another was Governor of the Netherlands in 1762, another a Marshal of Austria, another a Governor of Carinthia, another aide-de-camp to Franz Joseph. But probably the most important member of the clan of O'Donnell (sometimes one 'l' is dropped by the European branch of the family) was Marshal O'Donnell, one of the great soldier-politicians who took such a prominent part in the government of Spain. This O'Donnell occupied the curious but authoritative position during the Spanish War in Morocco in the mid-nineteenth century of Prime Minister, War Minister and Commander-in-Chief of the army. No doubt the political and military attachment was one of the great spurs that drove O'Donnell on in the war – he knew well that defeat in the field would also mean defeat in parliament. That he could not afford and with the price so high eventually brought the Moors to surrender, demanding, and receiving, full submission.

Outside Spain, all the best plumed generals of Europe about this time seemed to be of Irish extraction. Among them were the Nugents, the O'Kellys, the Walls and the great family of Walshes of Carrickmines in Dublin who between father and son commanded the Austrian Army in Turkey and were highly decorated, even by Poland. Not all belonged to the plumed brigade. Irish soldiers formed a great part of the regiments that fought in the War of the Succession, in the War of the Peninsula, in Spain's war in Morocco and in just about every civil strife of that land. Not that they won the same awards as their countrymen in France but then maybe the warmer climate had something to do with it – when not fighting they were finding that love was the best substitute for war. In Charles III's Irish Legion in Spain fought the Kennedys and Murphys and Kelleys and all these, according to the annals of the time, 'had several very beautiful Moorish maidens for wives'. So Spain provided suitable diversions for the fighting man, but she, and the other nations, asked the full price and the Irish soldier was generally placed first in line or held for the dirty end of the job. They paraded and marched and fought their way through so many campaigns that it would become a bore to list even an *nth* of them all. Indeed a full review of these men, herded like cattle from their own land, would be little more than a litany. Dean Swift knew them and all they meant when he wrote: 'I cannot too highly esteem these gentlemen of Ireland, who, with all the disadvantages of being exiles and strangers, have been able to distinguish themselves, in so many parts of Europe, by their valour and conduct above all nations.'

Swift might even have known of the Lacy family who set out in the seventeenth century to become the greatest leaders of fighting men who ever sailed from the country. No fewer than five from the one family figure in the military history of Europe – Marshal Lacy overran the Crimea in the service of Russia; Marshal Count Lacy, his son, was a distinguished general in the Seven Year War; Francis Anthony, Count de Lacy, was Captain General of Catalonia; his brother Patrick Lacy, Major of the Ulster Regiment in the Spanish service; and his son Louis Lacy fought bravely in the wars of the Peninsula and was *Chef-du-Battailon* of the Irish in 1807. All of them were descended from the Lacy family of County Limerick.

Before the Seven Years War was to echo with the name of Lacy the family name had become one of the most trusted in Russia. Peter Lacy began to fight early in life . . . at twelve he was in Sarsfield's army; at thirteen he was an ensign. With this start in life there could be no turning on the road for him. He travelled to France with the Athlone Regiment and served throughout the Italian campaign under Marshal Catinat. But being at heart a soldier of fortune he looked around him. Few countries were left where the spoils of war still held out a lavish hand but Lacy decided that for him there was a future in Russia. He certainly chose right and by thirty he commanded fifteen thousand men; he was soon a Brigadier-General; then General-in-Chief, eventually Governor. He fought for Russia in Sweden, in Poland and in Finland but his greatest exploits were against the Turks where he and the notorious Count Munich had some of the toughest battles of military history. Fighting against Lacy was the Khan of the Crimea, a fantastic, wild figure who could call on 100,000 men to fight for him at any time. He lived the life of a true Ottoman, had huge flocks, coined copper money, drew as revenue from one part of his empire twenty cart-loads of honey, and had as a personal guard green and purple clad, rugged Janissaries. Lacy's campaign against the Emperor began in

March 1736 when the Irishman marched on the city of Azoph. For twelve days the city held out and then Lacy marched in. All through the Crimea the great march went on and despite a poor finish to the complete operation Lacy's future was settled. He returned in glory and lived the life of a soldier to the end – certainly a financially happy soldier. When he died he left estate valued then at £60,000. His son carried on the family name and even up to the revolution one of his descendants held a governorship in Russia.

As cavaliers of fortune there could have been few examples as good as the Lacys but it took another Irishman to add the glamour touch to the story of the Gaels who served Russia. Out from the county of Leitrim in the early 1700s went a twenty-four-year-old fortune seeker from the family of O'Rourke. He headed for London and tried his hand at many a trade before he settled for the soldier's life. But he didn't last long in London; when it was discovered that he was a Roman Catholic he had to resign his commission. But to resign a commission was one thing, to resign yourself to the life of a lackey was another. O'Rourke followed the well-trodden Irish path and found himself in France where very soon he was given command of Louis XV's regiment of Royal Scots. But being a true born son of the Gael his feet soon developed the travelling itch and he headed for Poland. Here he was offered a commission in the army but it was so long in coming that O'Rourke found himself on the move again. Next stop was Russia. Here rewards were more quickly forthcoming and he was appointed First Major of horse cuirassiers in the Czar's Regiment of Bodyguard. When war with Prussia interrupted his royal household duties O'Rourke showed that there was plenty of fight in him. He distinguished himself everywhere he went and at the end of the war Frederick the Great sent for him to see who was this hero of so many war stories – a man who in a brief span was a legend for impetuosity and courage.

As the Prussians had committed so many outrages against the Russians, O'Rourke's fellow officers urged him not to go. 'It can only be a trap,' they argued. 'Once you are in Frederick's hands he will have you executed.' But the Irishman wouldn't accept this: 'Frederick was a brave enemy; only cowards murder; I'll go.' Fortunately O'Rourke was right and Frederick entertained him lavishly and talked to him about the war. He wondered what made even a mad Irishman think that the Russians could beat the Prussians, above all what made him think they could storm such an impregnable city as Berlin. 'In Russia,' replied O'Rourke, 'we obey the King no matter what we think. If he ordered me to scale the Heights of Heaven, I would immediately make the experiment.' Delighted with this dedication and to show just how much he thought of him Frederick presented O'Rourke with a diamond-studded sword.

After that the Irishman's wandering spirit was up again and leaving Berlin he went back to France where he was appointed Colonel of Horse, created a Count and invested with the Order of St Louis. At the commencement of the American War of Independence he went to London and offered his services to the British – but, as on so many occasions before and since, the English only treated the Irishman with scorn. There seemed little left to do now and O'Rourke made the great trek back to Russia where he died in 1782.

Possibly the English remembered the frequent mistakes they had made during the century by rejecting so many great Irish soldiers and when Lavall Nugent, a descendant of the Earl of Westmeath, came and offered his services in the 1800s he was quickly taken into the British army. Maybe it was a twinge of conscience but more than likely it was Nugent's reputation that dictated events. All over Europe he was known for his gallant conduct in the Austrian army. His bravery earned him a place as a Knight of the Military Order of Maria Theresa when he was only twenty-two. Promotions came with each battle and ten years later he had reached the rank of Major-General and also Plenipotentiary to the Congress which preceded Napoleon's marriage to Maria Louisa. Refusing to sign the terms of peace offered by Napoleon to Austria he went to England where he was immediately welcomed into the army with the rank of Lieutenant-General. But his heart was in Austria and after four years he went back again and played a leading part in pushing the French out of Italy. Although out of their service the British awarded him a KB; he then fought as Captain-General of the Neapolitan army; then back to Austria to head her forces through many wars. In 1849 he became Field-Marshal. But he was a fighter through to the end and he could still be found with Emperor Franz Joseph on various campaigns even in his eightieth year.

The Irish always had a great *gradh* for the Austrians; someone has suggested that it was the chance to fight on the side of a glamorous woman that sent them scarpering off there. They would not go to Frederick despite Prussian efforts to raise a regiment in Ireland – but they would go further afield to serve against him. It was from the day in 1740 when Frederick declared war on Maria Theresa that the real immigration began. It became almost as great a flow as that into France and at one time there were thirty Irish generals in the Austrian army, although there was never an Irish Regiment as such in the land. Again there is a long list of fighting families who settled down happily in Vienna and environs, notably the Laudons, Browns, Fitzgeralds, Nugents, O'Connells, O'Briens, Lacys and Taffees.

The theory that Maria Theresa herself may have had a winning effect on the Irish soldiers is given backing by the various stories that link her and the wanderers. A young man who had gone to Vienna to study theology was standing outside his college one day when the Empress passed by. Students were as vociferous then as they are today and he shouted at Marie Theresa.

'There's a fine young man who should be in my army,' she said to her aide-de-camp, Colonel Browne, another Irishman. 'What was he saying?' The Colonel had heard nothing but being as glib of tongue as he was of sword, replied: 'He said, Your Majesty, that he wished it was his luck to serve you.' The Empress immediately sent for the student and offered him a commission in one of her crack regiments. In less than a year he was a captain; gave up all thoughts of becoming a priest and still warrants a place in Austrian history today as Field Marshal Brady.

It had not always been the drawing power of a beautiful Empress that brought the Irish to Austria: in the seventeenth century a battalion of Irish Musketeers, commanded by Colonel Walter Butler, formed part of the Imperial Guard, while his brother James commanded a battalion of Irish dragoons. These two did more to influence Austria in favour of the Gael than any others. They had all the marks of soldiers of fortune – they were arrogant, brave, cunning, ruthless and courageous. In 1631 Walter, the younger of the two, defended Frankfurt against the victorious army of Gustavus Adolphus. At the head of eighteen thousand men with two hundred pieces of cannon and a pontoon bridge one hundred and eighty feet long, the King of Sweden marched against the town. The Austrian generals set up their defences and Butler was given the weakest parts of the walls to defend. 'Take him (Butler) in every respect,' wrote the historian of Gustavus, 'he was one of the bravest officers in the Emperor's service but as the Imperialists envied this gallant foreigner, care was taken to place him at the weakest part of the fortification.'

But Butler wasn't disheartened – a soldier had to fight whatever fate (or other generals) decided. The extraordinary thing is that all historians agree that Butler's post was almost incapable of being defended. Certainly Butler knew well just how weak his positions were and he told the commander so. But nobody would heed him and after a two-day siege, during which Butler wanted to attack the waiting Swedish and Scottish soldiers, his post was attacked. At the same time attacks were made on other parts of the city and soon the Imperial soldiers were on the run. At Butler's post the fighting was ferocious and even though Gustavus himself led the assault he could not break through. When one musketeer was dragged over the defences the king asked him: 'What soldiers are here?' 'Colonel Butler's Irish regiment,' came the reply. When Gustavus heard this he drew off his troops and they attacked a German-held position nearby. Three hours later they were through. Most of the Imperial generals took flight leaving the Irish to face the frightening wave of Swedes and Scots. Three Irish Lieutenant-Generals were killed, as well as various other officers and hundreds of men. But they still fought on with Butler at their head. Eventually he was hit by a bullet 'and had his sword arm broken by a musket-ball, and when he fell the remnant of his gallant soldiers surrendered and resistance was at an end'.

Meanwhile, everywhere the fleeing generals went they told the story that the Irish and Butler had let them down. 'He sold Frankfurt,' was their story and they pointed out that Butler wasn't dead and neither was he with them. Where else was he but with Gustavus? By an extraordinary stroke Butler was with Gustavus – carried to the king on a litter of pikes at the royal request, to a victory banquet. But it was as a vanquished officer that Gustavus wanted him. 'Cavaliers,' he told his officers, 'I will not eat a morsel until I have seen this brave Irishman of whom we hear so much.' When Butler was brought in with his escort of guards Gustavus looked at him: 'Sir, are you the elder or the younger Butler?'

'May it please your Majesty,' replied the wounded man, 'I am but the younger.'

'God be praised,' said the king. 'Thou art brave. But had it been the elder of your family I would have run my sword through you now, However go and let my physicians attend you.'

So Walter Butler was taken away, not knowing just what it was that had made his brother James so hated by the king, but as he lay injured at Frankfurt rumour reached him that the Imperialist defeat in the city was being blamed on him. He asked for help from Gustavus.

'Sir,' said the king, 'it is in my power to do your character ample justice and in such a manner that it can never be controverted. I will bear full testimony to your faith and valour under my own hand and royal seal.'

He then drew up one of the most remarkable documents ever produced by a ruler towards an enemy. In it he wrote that 'if the Imperial generals, instead of acting like poltroons, had performed but a fifth part of what this gallant Irishman had done, I should never have been master of Frankfurt, but after an obstinate siege alone.' He then had all his Swedish and Scottish generals sign the paper in his presence. Butler accepted the document and with the king of Sweden's blessings set off to the Emperor. But he made one or two calls on the way, dropping in on Imperial officers who were slandering him still. The first man he met, a Colonel Behem, he challenged to single combat on horse or foot, with sword or pistol. The Irishman's known skill and courage as well as the justice of his cause was enough for Behem – he signed a full retraction and apology. With these documents in his pocket Butler rode to Poland where he recruited his own regiment of cavalry, and returned in triumph to the Emperor. He became a great favourite of the court but never reached further promotion in the army.

Walter Butler's story ended quietly in Austria: not so that of his brother, James, who was to live on in history as the man who snared Wallenstein, the German dictator, when he became too ambitious for the Austrian Emperor's liking. Ferdinand authorised Butler and all his officers to withdraw their allegiance from General Wallenstein. Together with two Scots, Lesley and Gordon, James Butler organised a banquet for Wallenstein's supporters and even before the dinner had finished they had killed all the general's loyal friends. It was left to another Irishman, Captain Walter Devereaux, to kill Wallenstein. Breaking through the door into the dictator's bedroom the Captain was faced by Wallenstein standing in his shirt, pale but composed, and defenceless.

'Art thou the betrayer of Ferdinand and the Empire?' asked Devereaux, rushing towards the man. 'If so you must die.' Wallenstein made no reply but bared his breast and the Irishman killed him with one sword thrust. For their part in this gory piece of history both Butler and Devereaux were rewarded with gold chains which they were told to wear 'in memory of an emperor you have saved from ruin'. The other officers were suitably rewarded; some lived to enjoy their promotions but James Butler was killed a year later and left behind him a large fortune in Austria – and one of the most mixed historical assessments ever accorded to an Irishman.

But between the hero and the traitor there is very little in times of war. Often during the bitter seventeenth, eighteenth and nineteenth centuries men from the same town faced each other in different foreign armies, especially those of France and Austria. Who then was the hero or the traitor? Take Cremona, for instance, where the Irish on the side of France and clad only in their nightshirts fought off the might of Austria . . . but it was left to an Irishman on the Austrian side to take the great personal battle honours when he captured the French Field Marshal Villeroi. Lieutenant Francis MacDonnell was his name. Was he on the right side that day? This battle between right and wrong finally devolves on a personal opinion: certainly this was true of the 'Irish Brigade' which became involved in the internal strife between Victor Emmanuel and Pope Pius IX in 1860. Raised and financed purely in Ireland they took part in some very obstinate fighting, letting the Italians know that whenever an Irishman fights – whether the cause be right or wrong – he fights well. Faced in their one and only encounter on Italian soil by a much stronger and far better equipped force of Italians, the Irish somehow managed to stave off defeat for a while. Mauling, hand fighting and bayoneting they broke up the king's forces until at last the Italian commander asked for an armistice. It was granted, but then came a devastating wild rush on the band of Papal fighters by the Royal forces, a mixture of Austrians, French and Irish. From the thousands that set out less than three hundred were left after this offensive and O'Reilly, the Irish commander, was forced to surrender. It was a sad ending to a sad beginning. But for all that it had done nothing to lessen the reputation of the Irish in Europe; so many had fought, planned, commanded and died there that one unplanned excursion could not harm their name.

It was a large slice of Irish history that was written into the Continental stream of Gaels, but as one great door closed to Irish fighters others were opening. Far away was another continent ready to house the Irish emigrants: France and Europe for the glory of the seventeenth and eighteenth centuries, Australia for the sorting of injustices in the nineteenth, a place for rebellion rather than service.

CHAPTER 3

Eureka!

'THE IRISH TAKE to rebellion like ducks to water,' wrote an Englishman soon after the battle of the Eureka Stockade. He didn't add that down through the years they had been given plenty of practice in rebellion – and justification for trying to change the world around them. Wherever they went they were dogged by British rule and by the lack of foresight that often went with it. Certainly this was so in Australia where the British made enough mistakes in twenty years to rile every Irishman alive. The real mistake of the London Government was their belief that transportation of every rebel and criminal from England, Scotland, Wales and Ireland to Australia was going to clean up their own society. It didn't, of course, but it brought together a much stronger force of rebellion against them in Australia. The surprising thing then was not that rebellion came but that it wasn't a great deal worse.

From the day in January 1788 when the first fleet entered Botany Bay – and for many years after that – Australia became a land peopled with an extraordinary mixture of genuine and honest-to-God adventurers, felons, murderers, thieves, and politicians who had fallen out of favour, as well as a fair sprinkling of some of the most famous names in the history of Irish rebellion. Deportation became one of the most frightening threats of the time and of all the deportees in Australia from 1788 to 1800 over seventeen per cent came from Ireland; 28,900 Irish entered the country as immigrants in the two years 1853–54. Many of these were deported for their part in the various rebellions or driven out by the Great Famine. When all these mingled, with their hate of the British, there was certain to be an explosion.

There had been earlier rumblings, but they were rumblings only. Eureka was the great stand of the immigrants – and not only Irish – against Colonial misrule in Australia. It is accepted that it was one of the most symbolic events in Australia's history. Mark Twain commented:

> I think it may be called the finest thing in Australian history. It was a revolution – small in size but great politically; it was a strike for liberty, a struggle for a principle, a stand against injustice and oppression. It was the barons and John over again; it was Hampden and Ship-Money; it was Concord and Lexington; small beginnings all of them, but all of them great in political thinking; all of them epoch-making. It is another instance of a victory won by a lost battle. It adds an honourable page to history; the people know it and are proud of it. They keep green the memory of the men who fell at Eureka Stockade.

Eureka happened after gold was found in Ballarat in August 1851. Up to then it had been a pastoral area and Government officials who feared that the lands on which they had squatters rights would be overrun, would willingly have kept quiet about the gold find for ever. But a 'find' is something that can't be kept quiet; so the rush started. The law, at the time, was that all minerals found under the ground were the property of the Crown; the Government held it had a right to make a toll of any finds, so a licence fee of thirty shillings a month was imposed on all diggers. From the very beginning this licence (or Miner's Right as it was called) was not well received. The licence was in this form:

Gold Licence

No. 185

The bearer having paid the sum of one pound ten shillings on account of General Revenue of the Colony, I hereby license him to Mine or dig for Gold, or exercise or carry out any other trade or calling on such Crown Lands within the Colony of Victoria as shall be assigned to him for these purposes by any one duly authorised in that behalf.

This licence to be in force until or during the month of , and no longer.

Signature

Commissioner.

But if the licence annoyed the diggers the regulations that went with it were blood stirring. They laid down that the licence was not transferable, it had to be produced whenever demanded by any commissioner, peace officer, or other authorised person. Further it was always issued by the local police station and could only be used within half a mile of the police station from which it was issued. These regulations and the harsh way they were enforced eventually led to the confrontation between troops and diggers at Eureka.

In September, a month after the find at Ballarat, a new commissioner arrived and immediately began to ensure that everyone had a licence to dig. The diggers held a meeting and decided to ask the Commissioner to withdraw the licence fee. But they got their first taste of absolute administration. They were told that the Commissioner was there to administer the law and that was what he was going to do. And then he added:

'If you don't pay the fee I'll bloody well make you.' This was the spirit then established among the diggers of Ballarat, most of whom were Irish. Not the slightest trace of sympathy was shown by officialdom and digger-hunting became a favourite pastime for the police. Hardly a day passed in the diggings that men were not arrested and locked-up in 'the logs' (as the local jails were called). There they were fined because they had mislaid, lost or not renewed their licences. Often men who were not diggers were arrested because they could not produce licences and their word would not be taken by the unsympathetic officials and police cadets. The call that would send the diggers running was a hail of 'I say, you fellow, show me your licence' or 'Hello, you sir, show me your rights.' The most inhuman treatment was meted out to the diggers. Peter Lalor, an engineer from the midlands of Ireland, who eventually became the miner's leader, wrote:

> The diggers were subjected to the most unheard of insults and cruelties in the collection of this tax being in many instances chained to logs if they could not produce the licence. I have often known men to be asked for their licence four or five times in the course of a day . . . the water to be contended with in deep sinkings compels the diggers frequently to change their dress; in doing so they often leave their licence behind; under such circumstances should they be visited by the police, they are dragged, wet and dripping as they may be, to the prison, like common felons. The scarcity of gold made the diggers feel those evils more keenly.

The diggers tried to set up their own warning system and whenever the cry of 'Traps' or 'Joe, Joe' went up there was a wild stampede by the unlicenced ones to get down deep shafts or out of the way until the police had moved on. But they weren't often quick enough and the police seldom went away without a string of men handcuffed together. A contemporary commentator wrote: 'being servants of the crown they acted more arbitrarily than the Crown itself.'

Now and again when faced by the Crown the men found a way out – but few quite so glib as John Murphy who was arrested with Garrett Brennan on Jackass Flat in 1854 and brought before the magistrates. Both men had paid for their licences but had left them in their tents on the day. Murphy who was well known for his droll humour asked the magistrate: 'Would your honour have that fellow, that policeman there, fire on a man who had paid for his licence and left it in his tent, if he ran away after being rounded-up by the police?'

'I would not,' replied the magistrate.

'Then your honour, I'll leave you,' and Murphy, knocking out the policeman, jumped the fence and ran off into the bush at top speed. Brennan stayed on and was reprimanded.

The humour though was quickly going out of the situation. Timothy Hayes, called the Hibernian Orator, began a campaign to get the men together. His call at the miners' meetings, 'Will you fight for the cause, boys?' always brought a great roar of approval. And he followed this with: 'And will you die for the cause, boys?' The roar was even louder still, but, as one writer points out, when the fighting did start Hayes forgot that he was to die for the cause and he tamely surrendered. He was reproached for his temerity by his wife who 'was a much better soldier than Hayes'.

The authorities began to show the first signs of panic. They brought in two detachments of soldiers, the police stations in Ballarat were considerably strengthened. One group of soldiers marching past a camp was attacked by the miners; one was shot in the leg, others injured; diggers attacked the carts to get all the guns and ammunition they could. When word got out about the attack the miners' leaders strongly disapproved of these tactics . . . but blood was up, on both sides. Diggers burned their licences; they swore they would never pay for another one; they lit fires and roared approval. The next day, as if to make sure of a confrontation, the police, with soldiers and cavalry, marched into the diggings asking for licences. The miners shouted and booed, threw stones and a few shots were fired. Diggers were arrested. Peter Lalor, later asserted: 'A digger, who, I presume, had no licence, was running away, when an officer of police ordered his men to "fire on him" and "shoot him down", and he was fired at . . . the diggers believed that some of those in authority had come out that morning with the determination of having the diggers fired at.'

At this point the call went out for volunteers to gather with the diggers and defend themselves. The police withdrew, but the damage had been done. Lalor gathered five hundred men and he saw 'around me brave and honest men who had come thousands of miles to fight for independence'. He called on the volunteers to kneel down 'and with their heads uncovered, and hands raised to heaven, they solemly swore at all hazards to defend their rights and liberties. They promised to meet the next morning and then departed.'

The next morning was 1st December, the day the building of the Eureka Stockade began. A square plot of ground about an acre in all was fenced off with wooden slabs, supplemented by upturned carts, all held together by ropes. Defensively it held little and it was more an area in which the men could meet and drill. There were a few claims inside the barricades and also a few digger's holes. Lances and pikes were made in a blacksmith's shop in the arena. Although the police believed that, at the time, the stockade was commanded by a man named Vern it was in fact commanded by Lalor, a man of some twenty-five years, strongly built, rugged and six feet tall. His second-in-command was Alfred Black.

During the first two days of December most of the men drilled, others went scouting for arms and ammunition. Word was sent to other camps telling the miners what was afoot and asking for assistance. By the second evening, a Saturday, a fair supply of arms, pikes and lances were in the hands of the miners, while in Melbourne the Government were hastily printing wanted notices for both Lalor (they spelt it Lawlor) and Black. All the time the police in Ballarat expected an attack and when none came the military took matters into their own hands and an attack was mounted. At the time the military advance was made there were about two hundred men in the stockade. Stories tell of men walking out earlier in the evening after finding things too slack in their defences; others say detachments of men had gone to get food; Lalor himself said afterwards that he had given orders for many of the men to leave because there was not enough sleeping accommodation in the enclosure. When the first shots woke the men at three o'clock in the morning they hastily rushed to the defences and were soon shooting it out with the redcoats. Lalor said that there were about seventy men in the stockade with guns, twenty with pikes, thirty with pistols, but many of the men who had firearms had only one or two rounds of ammunition. This was borne out at the end of the battle when some of the guns were found to be loaded – not with ammunition but with quartz stones. In the attacking force were 276 military and police; when their first volley rang out five men were killed. The rebels were given orders to shoot at the officers and very soon Captain Wise of the 40th Regiment and Lieutenant Paul of the 12th were down; one dead, the other seriously wounded. Lalor stood in the centre of the stockade on top of a logged-up hole, shouting orders and encouragement at his men, but after only some ten minutes 'I received a musket ball (together with two other smaller bullets) in the left shoulder which shattered my arm.' Other rebel leaders were shot and soon the redcoats were confronted only by a row of pikemen. A brief but deadly encounter followed until the small band was scattered. The insurgents' flag was torn down and the battle won – or lost. The military set fire to all tents within the stockade, took 125 prisoners and then returned to camp. Inside the burning tents, it was alleged, wounded men were left to burn alive. A newspaper reporter with the *Geelong Advertiser* wrote after his visit to the stockade:

> I counted 15 dead . . . they all lay in a small space, their faces upwards, looking like lead. Several of them were still heaving, and at every rise of their breasts the blood spouted out of their wounds . . . or just trickled away . . . some were bringing handkerchiefs, others bed covering or matting, to cover up the faces . . . a sight for the Sabbath morning I implore Heaven may never be seen again! Poor women crying for absent husbands, and children frightened into silence.

How many actually died in the affair has never been determined; generally the accepted number of miners is in the region of thirty-five; on the military side one officer and four men. Among the dead were men from England, Scotland and Canada . . . but the biggest number was from Ireland. Hynes, Mullins, O'Neill, Donaghey, Quin, Quinlan, McGlynn and many others were in the list of Eureka dead.

Peter Lalor escaped, and was treated by a doctor who eventually had to amputate his arm. He then moved around keeping out of the way until an amnesty was granted to all involved in the rising. He became a leading politician and a minister in the

Government. When he retired he was voted £4,000 'for his distinguished services to the state'. Lalor's fight was justified by a commission set up to enquire into the Eureka Stockade; it decided that the miners were forced into rebellion by bad laws, harshly enforced – an old story to the Irish of the time.

CHAPTER 4

Wild Colonial Boy

The contribution Ireland made to Australia's fighting lore goes a lot deeper than Eureka. Peter Lalor, by his own words, never saw anarchy, bloodshed or plunder as the objects of the defence of the stockade; but the same cannot be said about the number of bushrangers who, while becoming almost Robin Hood-like, with the help of time, set many a record against themselves when they were alive and killing. In the roll-call of Ben Hall, Mad Dan Morgan, Johnny Gilbert, Jack Bradshaw, one name stands out over them all – Ned Kelly. There will be some Australians who will not agree that Kelly should be regarded as a national hero, but certainly he is a national folk hero. He arrived on the Australian scene at a time when the country was, in part, ready to accept him – dirt, killing and all. It was after Eureka, after the first blood letting of the Irish. Possibly, in his own way Kelly diverted some of the under-currents against the Irish away from something far greater. Kelly managed to defy the whole might of the land, waging war against police, laughing at their seemingly feeble attempts to capture him, killing off the informer who might have handed him over to the law – this was the real stuff of the folk hero. But what was Ned Kelly like? How did the Kelly gang operate? The answers are part of Australian and Irish history.

Ned Kelly was brought up in a household where rebellion was a word that would never have been used, simply because the family was so much a part of its meaning. His father had been a rebel in his own way and had spent some time in prison for cattle stealing, so when young Ned and his brother Dan were boys they felt that the police were dedicated to persecuting the family, watching and waiting to trap even the youngsters in moments of prank. They grew up with a gross dislike of lawmen.

The Kelly gang consisted of four – Ned and his brother Dan, Joe Byrne and Steve Hart – and between them they built up a legend in their own lifetime. Australians – mostly those with Irish backgrounds – saw the gang as symbols of their own hatred of bureaucracy; saw them as four brave lads, generous when they had it and resourceful when they hadn't. And Kelly himself attempted, and generally succeeded, in adding to the legend. His message to those whose life and property he threatened, was: 'I am a widow's son outlawed and my orders must be obeyed.' It was this touch of cheek that gave the ordinary town and country folk confidence in the gang, confidence to hide them from the law and to cover up their tracks at every opportunity.

Ned – who signed his frequent notes and letters to the public and police 'Edward' – asserted that it was the lying evidence of a policeman that sent him running in the first place. Up to that occasion in 1877 he had been in frequent trouble and it does seem likely that the police, even despite their generally corrupt ways at the time, were justified in suggesting that he was guilty of cattle stealing. Ned was twenty-four when Constable Fitzpatrick arrived at the Kelly homestead to arrest young Dan. Exactly what happened when he went into the house has never been fully authenticated. According to the constable Ned came charging into the house shooting and shouting, one bullet hitting the policeman's hand. Ned, of course, denied this but didn't wait to argue with the police or anyone else. With Dan he took to the bush and was soon joined by Byrne and Hart.

Less than a year after their escape they were in their first real battle, the one murderous encounter of their lives. Four policemen, Kennedy, Lonigan, McIntyre and Scanlon, disguised as diggers, set out to capture the Kelly gang, but at Stringybark Creek Ned picked up their trail and spotted who they really were. Inadequately armed to fight it out in a gun battle with the police, the gang decided to take the camp quietly. When they got there only two policemen were on duty, McIntyre and Lonigan. 'As we had only two guns,' wrote Ned, 'we thought it best to try and bail those (the two men) up, take their firearms and ammunition and horses and we could stand a chance with the rest of them . . . not wishing to take life we waited. McIntyre laid his gun against a stump and Lonigan sat on a log. I advanced, my brother Dan keeping McIntyre covered.'

Instantly Lonigan reached for his gun and Ned shot him through the head. McIntyre surrendered and the outlaws collected the guns and even filled a pipe for McIntyre and chatted with him as they waited for the other two constables to return. When these did ride into the camp the gang was almost taken by surprise. Kennedy as he dismounted saw Kelly and took a shot at him; Scanlon tried to gallop away but he was shot. McIntyre saw his chance jumped a horse and galloped off. Only Kennedy was left to fight it out with the four. As the policeman moved from tree to tree Ned Kelly counted how many shots he fired and when the policeman stopped to re-load Ned stepped out and fired his shotgun; as Kennedy staggered Kelly fired his revolver. 'I could not help shooting them or else let them shoot me,' wrote Kelly, 'which they would have done had their bullets been directed as they intended them.'

The killing of the three policemen drew the whole might of

the Government of the State of Victoria against the gang. But with the elusiveness of the Scarlet Pimpernel Ned was always a good Kangeroo hop in front of the law. He knew the bush so well that he could tell in plenty of time when anyone came too near to his hiding place; then he slipped off to another. And he could still count on hundreds of farmers and prospectors in the northern part of the state and in New South Wales keeping him up to date with all the news.

But Kelly knew that he would have to do something other than just keep the people happy with stories; money was much better than legend to preserve loyalty. To get money to give to those in need the four of them raided the National Bank of Euroa. As one of them handed a cheque in over the front counter the others slipped in the back way and got away with £2,000. It was so easy that the trick was repeated at Jerilderie. This time the gang added a touch of sophistication; they locked the police in their own cells, donned their uniforms, herded the inhabitants into a pub, presented a written statement why they were doing the job . . . then they rode off with £2,100.

The cheek of this raid began to seal the Kelly legend; it was the talk of the countryside and soon the ballad-makers had written their version:

When they robbed the bank in Euroa town
You said they'd be run down,
But now they've robbed another one
This one's in Jerilderie town.

And the chorus to this song was the acclamatory 'Long may they reign, the Kellys, Byrne and Hart.'

No bushranger in history had really got to so many people in such a way; Kelly put his story across so well that he came to be seen as a man with a genuine grievance against authority; a man who was always courteous; who was a bit of a wit; who helped the poor and the needy and never saw his friends stuck for money or other assistance. He had built up a great army of sympathisers and by now the reward money for the gang's capture (it had started at a mere £500) was over £8,000.

At any time Byrne or Hart, or even Dan, could have turned crown evidence and the law would no doubt have pardoned them – Ned was the man they really wanted. Every effort was made to track him down; black trackers, aboriginals who could tell by the slightest disturbance of the earth whether anyone had passed that way, were brought into the hunt. And one man, Aaron Sherritt, a boyhood friend of Byrne, overawed by the amount of the reward, decided to sell the gang. But, inevitably word got to Kelly. He sentenced Sherritt to death and sent Byrne and Dan off to carry out the execution. He followed this by an expedition to the town of Glenrowan where he set about pulling up the railway tracks in an effort to wreck a police train that was due to hot up the Kelly hunt. Again it was the local hotel that was commandeered to hold the local townsfolk and in his usual way Ned set out to impress his captive audience. He told them why he had been first sent into the bush and what he was going to do in Glenrowan that very day. They listened, as just about every audience had, to Kelly – all except one man. He was listening and playing the friend for another reason. His name was Curnow, the local schoolmaster, and on the pretext that he would be better employed at home he persuaded Kelly to let him go. As courteous as ever Ned agreed with the schoolmaster's request, but this time he was tricked. Curnow got a red scarf and ran along the line with it tied around a lamp to warn the approaching train.

The train was stopped, the police warned and the deathtrap situation reversed. Even at this late stage Ned and his gang could have escaped. Ironically the one thing they hoped would save them was to be their downfall. For some time before Glenrowan Ned had been having sets of armour made from ploughshares. One inch thick, and incredibly heavy, they were hammered into rough helmets and jackets for the four men. Not even Ned could really have been naïve enough to expect these to provide absolute protection; their weight alone cut a man's mobility to nil. But his cockiness outweighed his sense and when he heard the train stop up the line he could have ordered the gang to get away. His own explanation later was that a bolt in his armour broke and he stopped to mend it; certainly he stopped too long. The police surrounded the hotel and began to fire. Ned was hit twice, in the foot and in the left arm. He ordered everyone in the room to lie down while he answered the siege. With his own injuries he could not fire so he decided to make a break for it and bring in some friends to help out the others. But when he got out he stumbled, fell and could not move. All night long he lay there as gun answered gun in the siege.

Inside, the people were being hit by the erratic fire of the police for by this time there was panic outside as well as inside; the police had even sent orders to Melbourne for a cannon to be brought in. It was only a matter of time; Byrne was the first to be shot; as he lifted a glass to his lips a bullet hit him below the armour and ripped up through his groin. Dan and Hart still fought on.

Then one of the most astonishing pieces of savage courage was enacted. Ned Kelly getting back some strength, pulled himself and his fantastic armour from the ground and began to stagger towards the police. Confronted by this huge black figure with a squared off head the police were stunned. Again and again they fired only to hear their bullets ricochet away into the night. Then from inside the mask came the unmistakable voice of Kelly roaring to his gang: 'Come on boys and we'll whip the lot of them together.' But the fight was gone from the two lads still in the hotel and Ned didn't last long; bullets zipped through his legs and groin. The police weren't finished yet; they continued to fire at the hotel; then they decided to let the people away but to burn out Dan and Hart. They watched the building burn to rubble but only when they walked through the charred remains did they find the two – side by side – having shot each other simultaneously rather than have the police take them.

It was reported by one of the newspaper artists sent to sketch the scene that when the mask was taken off Ned Kelly, the outlaw's face was bruised and cut where the bullets had hit the metal, but he still managed a grin: 'It was better than Waterloo, wasn't it, fellers?'

It was inevitable that Kelly would hang for his crimes but the surprising thing was that thousands of signatures were put to a petition asking for his pardon. They didn't help and a judge, who, it is said, was in a hurry to get to the races, quickly pronounced death. Kelly's final speech must have upset his plans – with passion the outlaw declared: 'I don't fear death. I fear it as little as to drink a cup of tea . . . let the hand of the law strike me down as it will but I ask that my story be heard and considered – not that I wish to avert any decree the law may deem necessary to vindicate justice or to win a word of pity from anyone. If my lips teach the public that men are made mad by bad treatment, and if the police are taught that they may exasperate to madness men they persecute and ill treat, my life will not entirely be thrown away. . . .' Then he warned the judge that the day was not far distant when they would meet again in another world – and the judge died shortly after the execution. Finally as he was being taken out from the courtroom he told everyone that one day 'I will return from my grave to fight'. He met his mother once before he died on the scaffold and his last words before he dropped are said to have been : 'Such is life. . . .'

With the elimination of the Kelly gang, bushranging in Australia – except for very minor outbreaks – practically disappeared. And when it ceased, an eventful century ended for the country: the diggers, the digger-hunting, the Eureka Stockade, the bushrangers, the Ned Kelly gang . . . and, finally, exactly one hundred years after that first fleet entered Botany Bay Peter Lalor died, and the part of the fighting Irish had been written large into the history of the land.

CHAPTER 5

Soldier he may be . . .

The reputation of the Irish as settlers and rebels, bushrangers and soldiers was solidly fixed in the world's eye. But if they were such good fighters on land what were they like on the sea? Somehow their escapades there had been passed over, lost in the welter of land actions and wars. It is true that you could sail the seven seas tomorrow and never see an Irish ship, but by the same token you could hardly cross a duckpond without meeting an Irishman.

Soldier he may be – but there is a trait in the Hibernian make-up that sends many a man scuttling off to sea as if every ancestor of his had been conceived in Davy Jones's Locker. Samuel Lover once suggested that the great attraction of the sea for the Irishman was 'its dark depths – its flashes of light – its terrible energy – its sportive spray – its striking alternations of frowning storm and smiling calm because they reflect the Irishman so vividly, that one would think it his peculiar element'.

There have been other great writers and seafaring men who would never have agreed with Lover – in many books the Irishman goes down as a bad sailor. But still others would fill a navy with Irish. Collingwood, Nelson's co-mate, told a recruiting officer: 'Don't send me any lubbers; but if you can get me some more of those Irish lads you sent me – they were all fine fellows, and are now top-men, every one of them.' As fine a testimonial as any seafaring man could ask.

And in the annals of the sea the sailors with the way of the blarney and the fighting spirit are to be found in plenty. The Father of the American Navy was Barry from the County Wexford; the Father of the Argentinian Navy was Brown from Westport in Mayo; the most audacious defeat that the British Navy ever received was handed out by a group of oar-pulling Irishmen; even Captain Bligh had his troubles from an Irish sailor; one became king on his own Pacific island – and who would dare to say the Irish are no sailors when they see the little black currachs fighting monster fish off the coast of Connemara?

Take a look first at what a bit of cheek will do for a man when luck is on his side and courage is on his cards. It was in the American Revolution that the British sent their warship *Margaretta* along New England's coast in the belief that a show of power would give heart to the loyal colonists and a warning to any rebels. Somehow it didn't quite work out that way. One of the ports of call was Machias Bay, Maine, where a man named Maurice O'Brien lived with his five sons. Maurice, a Corkman through and through, watched with interest as the man-o'-war dropped anchor. And only an Irishman with a streak of devilment in him could have dreamed up – and carried through – such a fantastic scheme.

Calling on a group of his neighbours O'Brien organised a trip out into the bay to have a look at the *Margaretta* – but every man in the convoy of little rowing boats knew what was really intended.

They were going to capture the British warship!

The captain of the big ship could not have even guessed what was in O'Brien's mind and when the colonists arrived beside his ship and hailed it he helped them aboard. Then he got his shock. O'Brien told him he was no longer in command – the ship was being taken into the American Navy!

The men from Maine took complete command and a shattered British naval command eventually got the message that one of their leading man-o'-wars had been captured. It was only to be expected that they would make an effort to get the ship back and at the same time make O'Brien pay for his audacity. So they sent out two more big ships – the *Diligence* and the *Tapnaguish* – to pay off the score. Result: The O'Briens were ready – and the British lost two more vessels!

The formal handing over from the O'Brien family was not long delayed and Maurice's eldest son, Jeremiah, sailed the squadron to Waterville where the provincial congress was being held. The congress showed their pleasure by giving Jeremiah a commission and placed him under the command of Wexford born John Barry, the man who has been hailed as the father of the US Navy.

Barry was a seaman from boyhood and was captain of the *Black Prince*, one of the largest vessels trading between London and Philadelphia when the war started. Washington knew well the value of having top sailors on his side: 'In any operation,' he once wrote, 'and under any circumstances a decisive naval superiority is to be considered as a fundamental principle, and the basis upon which every hope of success must ultimately depend.' Barry's value to him then was very high.

Certainly the seaman from Wexford soon proved himself and in the first naval engagement of the war he scored a crucial victory when he captured the British tender, *Edward*. Later he became a national hero when he set out in O'Brien-like fashion with only a few men in rowboats and captured an armed schooner. He became very much a force to be reckoned with and in mid-Atlantic added to American successes when he took command of two British cruisers. He was raised to the rank of Commodore and given the task of general supervision of the US Navy.

Setting off in a rowboat to capture a man-o'-war takes some beating, but it is typical of the Irish at sea. Some have commanded ships and fought battles for the United States, others have managed to come through some hazardous associations and battles in other parts of the world. William Brown, for instance, managed to survive capture by an English press-gang and eventually desert the British Navy to become commander of the Argentinian Navy that defeated Spain in battle after battle . . . when he died he was Admiral and supreme commander of the navy.

There are various statues to both Brown and Barry throughout the world; there isn't one to His Majesty O'Keefe, as daring and cunning an Irishman as ever sailed the seas – especially those around the Carolines.

O'Keefe established such a reputation that he even had his own flag flying between those of Spain and Germany when a dispute arose over who really owned the island he was living on. His full name was David Dean O'Keefe, six foot four, red haired with a mighty flowing beard . . . but to everyone in the South Seas he was the King of Yap, Monarch of Mapia, Sovereign of Sonsoral or just plain Majesty O'Keefe.

O'Keefe's story is that of a Robinson Crusoe who struck it rich. He was the only survivor of the shipwreck that landed him eventually on the Island of Yap in the Carolines. He got there in the roundabout way most sailors find their place on earth. Like most Irishmen he left Ireland for want of something better to do, became skipper of a coaster and made a hazardous living in the game of blockade running in the American Civil War. He was regarded as one of the toughest coaster skippers in his area and as if to prove it he hit a drunken sailor so hard one night that to all intents the sailor was dead. Not a man to tangle with the laws of the time, which could send even a skipper to walk the plank or dangle from a tree, O'Keefe took the first job that came his way – as mate on a ship that was sailing far away from Georgia. Away he went and it was years before he heard that the sailor hadn't died after all; in fact was as right as rain the next day with nothing more than a sore head to show for the night before.

That obviously was not the best time of O'Keefe's life for he wasn't long on his new ship before they ran into a tropical storm and sank on a coral reef. The only one to step ashore was the man from Sligo.

No man though could have asked for a better place to be shipwrecked – everything he needed was provided by nature: food, clothing and shelter. Even the natives were friendly; they believed in living the simple life of singing, dancing, love making, with only the occasional and very short tribal war to disturb the perfect peace. If anything other than this interfered with the balanced existence of the natives of Yap, it was likely to be their local currency – stone discs from one to twelve feet in diameter. The native with a good store of these could be considered a wealthy man – a wealth he wasn't likely to lose easily. One traveller wrote: 'When it takes four strong men to steal the price of a pig, burglary cannot but prove a somewhat disheartening occupation.' Not only was their size an advantage but they were also very scarce and therefore a perfect form of barter: they could only be obtained from an island four hundred miles away. Even then the native in search of his fortune had to hack them from the cliffs, and still paddle his canoe or raft back home through dangerous seas. Altogether an exhausting, dangerous but nevertheless wide-open business.

O'Keefe spotted the possibilities and he sailed for Hong Kong where he managed to get command of a junk, which, though old and decrepit, was to make his fortune. He sailed to the island of discs, quarried a whole load, and went back to trade with the natives of Yap. So intrigued were they with the Irishman's hoard that they were soon in a bartering mood – swapping coconut copra and *bêche-de-mer* for the discs. Then off sailed the bold D D O'Keefe to China to sell the goods and make the first big profit in his life.

But a heaven and a trading position like this were not likely to last a lifetime, word soon got out about the King of Yap's prosperous line of business. The first one to try and dethrone him was an Irish-American pirate named 'Bully' Hayes. O'Keefe went out to meet the pirates on their own ship and told Hayes where to take himself. Then, to show that the punch he once threw in Georgia was no fluke, he floored Hayes with one straight left and a following right. Hayes got the message and sailed off to find his own paradise.

O'Keefe realised then that some sort of local defence force was needed so on his next trip to Hong Kong he bought three or four cannon and some more arms. When he got back he set the cannon on his front lawn and recruited the first Yap army – forty or so Sonsoral natives. He trained the natives and when they were ready to fight he flew his own flag – a shamrock and coconut design with his own initials embroidered into it.

His Majesty O'Keefe reigned undisturbed for almost a dozen years, then the first efforts were made by Spain to claim the island: they sent a garrison and governor. But Germany had similar designs, they sent a garrison and a governor, and very soon there were three flags flying at the harbour of Yap – the Spanish, the German, and O'Keefe's. Eventually the question of who owned the island was put to Pope Leo XIII and in 1885 he confirmed the Spanish ownership. The Germans went but not O'Keefe. He was there first and anyway the Spaniards were not causing him any trouble, and as far as they were concerned he was a pleasant enough fellow. They got on very well – for another ten years – then America and Spain got to grips in war. The Spanish asked for O'Keefe's surrender but with the tongue that had first charmed the natives of Yap, O'Keefe talked himself out of trouble and when the war was over and America had won, the bearded king received a surrender – from the Spanish Governor.

But destiny would never allow a man to live in such harmony. Behind his back Spain sold the island to Germany and back came a garrison by orders of the Kaiser. Not even O'Keefe's cannon or Sonsoral guard could stop it this time, but nevertheless O'Keefe flaunted his flag in their face, kept his bodyguard and occasionally threatened them with all the fury his red-bearded frame could muster. Somehow they never came to blows and it was left to the sea to finish off the story it began almost half a century before. On a May day in 1900 the King of Yap sailed in his ship, the *Santa Cruz*, into one of the worst typhoons the Pacific had ever seen. Neither the good Captain O'Keefe nor the *Santa Cruz* were ever seen again.

It was no doubt the way that O'Keefe would have died if he had been given the choice, for like another Irishman in the faraway island of Samoa he went out fighting. O'Keefe, however, was a very different character from Tom the Devil. No one ever knew whether Tom was a shipwrecked sailor or a runaway convict. But wherever he came from Tom had his head screwed on right and it wasn't long before he became a great favourite among the natives on the island of Manono. After showing what he could really do in a rough and tumble, Tom got the reputation of being a man who shouldn't be tangled with. In local tribal wars they called him the Devil – and then to give the Devil his due they paid complete homage to the Irishman, making him a chieftain. Everything was made easy for Tom; his food and home were provided and he had the freedom of all the girls in the tribe – which he ought to have realised was going to get him into no end of trouble. One day the inevitable happened – Tom had been taking his pleasures too often and there was a general uprising among the young men and girls. A group of girls got Tom into a pleasant grove with a pleasant promise and got him into an awkward predicament. When he was involved in a loving tangle there was a combined assault from all the young men of the village. As he was clubbed to death his last words were: 'My club! My club!'

Which, as they say in Ireland, was a desperate way to go.

There must have been something in the Irish sailors' make-up that made them dream of being king of an island. When they achieved their ambition most of them governed well and they generally seem to have been highly thought of by their people. Today there are still descendants of many of these Irish wanderers on Pacific islands, the prime example being the two square mile island of Pitcairn.

There is a tablet on the wall of a house in Pitcairn: 'Sacred to the memory of Mr John Adams who died 5th March, 1829, aged 65 years.' It could add a lot about Adams, but it is said that the people still carry Adams around in their eyes – some seven per cent of the islanders even today having his blue eyes. He was their great leader; one historian has said that on the island of Pitcairn Adams gave the world the one and only real example of a golden age.

He was born at Enagh in County Derry, and his life was changed the day he signed on under Captain Bligh on the *Bounty*. He signed under the name of Alexander Smith and was not the only Irishman in the fifty-man crew – beside him was Micky Byrne, a blind fiddler. They sailed around the Cape of Good Hope and eventually reached Tahiti. But Bligh's harshness soon had the crew up in arms. In one of the sea's great mutiny stories Bligh was deposed; the militant crew made sure that as many as possible took part in their mutiny – even going so far as to thrust a bayonet into Adams's (Smith to the crew) hands. Bligh was astounded that the Irishman should have sided against him: 'Smith,' he raged, 'I wouldn't have believed it of you.'

Bligh was put off to fight his own battle in a small boat and the mutineers, many of whom had taken Tahitian wives, and with the crew supplemented with Tahitian men, sailed on . . . and on . . . and on . . . looking for a place where they could land and live. One day the old volcano neck of Pitcairn loomed out of the sea as they progressed between New Zealand and Panama. When they landed there were nine mutineers and their Tahitian wives, six Tahitian men and three wives, and one girl – twenty-eight in all. Then, almost as a sacrifice to the newfound land, they burned their boat. But even a Pacific paradise could not bring peace. The Tahitian men murdered most of the white men; the Tahitian women murdered the Tahitian men – and eventually only three white men and the women remained. One of these, Mathew Quental, threatened the lives of the other two – John Adams and Edward Young – so for the good of the greatest number Quental was killed. Then Young died of asthma, leaving only the women and Adams.

For twenty years Adams and his harem lived happily on the island; no one knew about them until one day an American whaler, *Topaz*, discovered the colony. The promise of a better civilisation took the Adams colony four thousand miles away to Norfolk Island but they did not like it there and soon returned to Pitcairn. According to the laws of Adams there was no tax on the island except sixpence for anyone who wished to keep a gun, but a penalty of £15 was imposed on anyone killing a cat – because of a plague of rats.

Adams had to fight through a terrible cruise on the *Bounty* and then the murder of most of his friends and shipmates to find a paradise. He became father, minister, ruler of the colony and was, according to all accounts, a devout and fair man whose memory is still honoured in the Pacific.

CHAPTER 6

The Rajah from Tipperary

ALL THE TALK about the Hibernian love of the sea would have been wasted in the case of Tipperary-born George Thomas. He took to the sea – but found that fame and fortune were more easily acquired on land.

There can't have been many Irish deserters from the British Navy who became Rajahs in India and virtual dictators of a large part of that country. But Thomas achieved this. Born in the mid-eighteenth century he was destined to be one of the most romantic, daring adventurers that ever set out from Ireland.

He joined the British Navy when he was just a boy and by the time he was twenty-five had risen to the rank of quartermaster. He was the sort of lad who always had an ear to the ground hoping for the break that was finally going to sever connections with the life that his family led on a small farm, under the stern thumb of the English in the Golden Vale of Ireland. He had no great love for his lords and masters in Tipperary and he saw in the navy a way to get to a place where a man could still find adventure and make a fortune. The land he was seeking was India where ruling princes paid handsomely for mercenaries willing and able to train and lead their armies.

One day when the man-o'-war, on which he was serving, anchored off Madras, Thomas made a break. Leading a small party on to land he went into hiding and as far as the British Navy was concerned Quartermaster George Thomas was just another deserter, one of the many who, over the years, had hopped ship in India. This deserter, however, knew exactly what he wanted and it wasn't long before he found himself building a reputation among the small private armies. His fighting qualities became legend and his knowledge of military tactics put him more often than not on the winning side in the perpetual tribal wars. But he wasn't satisfied in these achievements; he became expert in the local dialects and customs and very soon he was found in Delhi, seeking a more suitable employer. It was a knowledgeable man who could pick correctly in this part of India – the centre of Mohammedan intrigue and capital of the great Moguls.

With a typical Irish eye for measuring up the greatest chance he turned up at the court of one of the most notorious and beautiful widows in the land. Her name was the Begum of Sardhana, a one-time dancing girl. She had been married to another European adventurer, a callous fighter who became known as Somru Sahib. Somru was another one wanting to keep out of the way of the British; he had been involved in various battles with them and after one particularly brutal massacre was elevated to Rajah and given control of the province of Sardhana. When he died in 1778 his widow took over the government of the province. Soon she became as notorious as her husband and with the almost necessary mixture for a ruler of the times – bravery and cruelty – she led her own small army to many victories. The sight of her riding a white charger filled her people with more fear than love.

Then Thomas arrived . . . the tall, good-looking Irishman with the charm of tongue, fighting reputation, knowledge of the country, its lore and people. Flattery was his main weapon and the Begum, who was only thirty, fell for it. She gave command of her armies to the soldier from Tipperary and very soon he had established himself and won the respect of the men. India at the time was seldom without some sort of war – like the Irish, if they weren't fighting the British they were fighting among themselves – so he soon got the chance to show just how good a leader he was. An attempt was made to depose the ruling prince of Delhi and he sent to the Begum for help. Quickly the army of Sardhana was on the scene and, led by Thomas, they routed the attackers. It was just another step in the fame-making process of George Thomas – the Shah gave him a fortune and the delighted Begum made him Grand Vizier. But at the same time she would have been a lot happier making him her own Rajah, and no doubt she would have succeeded but for the fact that Thomas fell in love with her adopted daughter.

As if he were out to prove that all the old sayings about the Irish were very true, Grand Vizier Thomas with his own personal streak of obstinacy showed that you can't cross an Irishman in love and get away with it. Convinced of his own power he defied the Begum and married the girl. Thomas expected the Begum's jealousy to show through but he was sure that he had the complete backing of her army – the Begum knew it as well. Lurking in the background was the inevitable villain, a Neapolitan adventurer named Levassoo. He married the Begum and together they set out to plan the assassination of the Irishman: one for revenge, the other for power. But again Thomas came off on the right foot; he heard of the plot and quickly took himself and his wife out of Sardhana. And with him went his own personal cavalry regiment.

Now instead of wandering the country and offering just his own services Thomas had an army to offer for hire as well; and the first man to take him into service was an enemy of the Begum.

She owed great debts to the small kingdom and in a series of swift raids Thomas got enough plunder to make war between the two of them inevitable. Now it was Levassoo against Thomas and the odds looked very heavily in favour of the Rajah of Sardhana – but he reckoned without the reputation of Thomas. As soon as the Rajah's troops heard whom they were to fight they mutinied, and marched back to the capital with Levassoo in captivity. Before setting out to battle, the Rajah and Begum had made a pact that if either one was captured or killed the other would commit suicide, so when confronted with her captured husband the Begum pretended to plunge a dagger into her heart. Levassoo, believing she had killed herself, grabbed a pistol from a guard and shot himself.

The soldiers – probably astounded by the whole performance – locked the Begum in her palace until they could sort out the next-in-line problem. Somehow she managed to get a message to Thomas imploring him to help her. As the recorder of the story tells 'he came and with great chivalry as it is known among the Irish' he talked her people into reinstating her.

Then off he went – this time to look for a kingdom of his own. Less than a hundred miles from Delhi was the province of Hariana, where various tribes had been fighting amongst each other for years over who should be the ruler. This was where Thomas headed and without very much trouble he took over the capital, Hansi, and installed himself as Rajah. The need for power grumbled at him all the time and soon he set out to conquer the whole Punjab, taking on the might of the great Sikh armies. And again he won, beating off the much stronger armies time and time again and eventually forcing the Sikhs to pay him dues of some two million rupees. He became a virtual dictator of the whole land.

It was a position he wasn't likely to be allowed to hold for very long and various other chiefs came to the side of the Sikhs. At one battle Thomas's army was outnumbered by over two thousand men but he still managed to thrash the attackers. By now a much wider area of the country had become involved and more men were brought up to attack the Irish Rajah of Hariana, including the army of the ungrateful Begum. But it was a personal tragedy that was the downfall of Thomas. His young wife was killed, and the despair of the Irish settled on him. Morose, and drinking far too much, he allowed the attacking forces to regroup and bring in new men. Suddenly his troops were thrown into another furious battle. This time they lost and Thomas only gained his fortress at Hansi just ahead of the following tribesmen. Surrounded by hostile tribesmen and a great army commanded by a Frenchman there was little hope for Thomas, but equally there seemed little chance of the attackers ever getting him out. As the siege dragged on and on efforts at a compromise were made. The French commander offered Thomas freedom if he surrendered and promised him a completely unhampered journey away from the province. He also promised that no attempt would be made to take away the great personal fortune amassed by the forty-five-year-old Irishman. Terms were agreed, a great banquet was held by his enemies in honour of Thomas, and then the former Rajah marched away to the neutral territory of the British East India Company.

For all his power and ability Thomas still had a great longing to get back to Ireland. He set out on the journey home but he had not got very far when he was struck down with fever and died at Berhampore on 20th August 1802. There had, and have, been other Irishmen in India but they never achieved the personal glory of the Rajah from Tipperary.

CHAPTER 7

The Ould Reliable

'TELL ME THIS,' queried an American friend one day, 'if you really hate the English so much why do you fight for them'? On the face of it there are many answers from the 'Well, it's all a case of geography' to the more facile 'And why wouldn't we fight for England and her paying us for it'? In between the two answers rise the real complexities of the situation. How can one justify a nation that has cursed England, cheered her every woe and then when the chips were really down goes out and helps her to win the war?

Possibly we can put it down to old habits dying hard. The Vale of Tamar is littered with the bones of the Irish who died helping Harold rid England of the Norman invader; and just about every other battle that England has fought has seen Irishmen in there fighting with just as much fervour as if they were fighting for their own. In Edward's war against the Scots in 1333 Maurice, first Earl of Desmond, led the attack at Halidon Hill; in the war against the French, 1347–56, the same Maurice, accompanied by Maurice Fitzgerald, fought so well that they were commended by the king; at Agincourt 'with lank-lean cheeks and war-worn coats, presenting them unto the gazing moon so many horrid ghosts' they gave history a chance to realise what the impetuosity of an Irish charge really is; in the Wars of the Roses they were on the side of Lancaster while York too had its share according to Shakespeare:

The Duke of York is newly come from Ireland:
And with a puissant and a mighty power,
Of gallowglasses and stout kernes,
Is marching hitherward in proud array.

John of Lincoln, Perkin Warbeck, had places for the Irish too; 'gallowglasses, grim of countenance, tall of stature, big of limb'.

So possibly it was there in the blood and flowed right through to the men whose names will be for ever remembered with the English – Wellington, Moore of Corunna, Nicholson of Delhi, Colonel Kelly of Chitral, right through the illustrious regiments and battalions of Inniskilling Dragoons, Dublin Fusiliers, Connaught Rangers, Irish Guards and many, many others to Montgomery of Alamein.

It comes as no little surprise to many English to be told that so many of their great leaders and men were in fact Irish born. Wellington is a prime example of this. He has been dubbed 'the archtype of the stern, silent Englishman' and yet he was born in Dublin from a family line that was as Irish as the Butlers or the Geraldines. Born Arthur Wesley at 24, Upper Merrion Street, Dublin, in 1769 he changed his surname, as did the rest of the family to Wellesley twenty-seven years later. He was a shy sensitive lad – hardly the right sort to be sent off on an army career but he soon proved emphatically that he had the guts to see him through all the rough times. First at Flanders, then to India and eventually a knighthood – Sir Arthur Wellesley.

Then with a great sweep of war Sir Arthur found his place in history. He took command of the Allied Armies against Napoleon in Portugal and Spain, and the long dogged struggle ended with victory for him. Then onwards to the final great flourish of his career – Waterloo. A battle that had him commenting: 'Thank

God, I do not know what it is to lose a battle . . . but certainly nothing can be more painful than to gain one with the loss of so many of one's friends.' These are feelings that have been re-echoed by so many great soldiers at the moment of victory – but from Wellington a man of few words they spoke volumes. He had knocked the cocked hat from the head of Napoleon in a fierce encounter. He didn't hand out bouquets at the end of it all but once burst out that it was not likely to have been such a victory if he hadn't been there. He wasn't a man to ladle out praise but no doubt the fact that almost half his army was made up of Irish did not fail to pass his notice.

And so on like will-o'-the-wisps through the years of history the Irish found themselves on England's side in many a battlefield encounter – de Lacy Evans, Viscount Gough, Major-General Sir Robert Rollo Gillespie, Lord Napier, Sir Edward Michael Pakenham – a tremendous list of Irish-born leaders.

The trouble, indeed, with the link between Ireland and England is that it was forged so strongly that to take just one of the links is almost taking unfair advantage of the others. The regiments themselves that spilled out through the years – Dragoons, Horse, Hussars, Guards, Rifles, Rangers, Fusiliers – camped on many a foreign field with a name from Ireland as a prefix. But it wasn't just to the known Irish regiments that Irishmen found their way – frequently they could be found mixed up with companies and groups of the oddest associations. Generally this was a result of a strange regiment being posted in Ireland. One prime example was the Fourth Regiment of Horse. In the *Dublin Penny Journal* of 1832 an 'eye witness' wrote about this extraordinary regiment in which his five grand-uncles had served. He remembered their uniform:

> these old spolia have a different cut and character from the golden gauds that decorate our modern chivalry. Why, sir,

> the old iron helmet crested with red horse hair, would weigh down the head of one of our present striplings, while the basket hilted Andrea Ferrara would sprain the wrist of a modern pretty officer. To be sure my grand-uncles were not sons of noblemen, who chose the army, *pour passer le temps*, but sons of an Irish gentleman who had nothing to give them but their swords, and thus sent them to win their way through the world, like true Irishmen by fighting those whom they never saw before and cutting away right and left all before them.

This regiment had been in Ireland for thirty years – from the conclusion of Queen Anne's wars to 1742 – and naturally brought into its ranks local men. One historian recorded that he did not recollect at any time more than 'two or three private men in it of any other country'. Made up eventually of members of old Irish families it wasn't uncommon for a man to give from twenty to thirty guineas for a trooper's place. The rest of the army eventually taunted the Black Horse, commanded by Sir John Ligonier, as the Virgin Mary's Guards because of the overwhelming number of Catholics in its ranks.

When the regiment was hurriedly drafted home to prepare for France it was caught on the hop – uniforms were due to be replaced in a matter of weeks and horses were in pretty poor condition. So poor was their turnout that the king on reviewing them at Hounslow said to their commanding officer, 'Ligonier, your men have the air of soldiers, despite their clothes. Their horses indeed look very poorly, how is this?'

'Sir,' replied the Colonel, 'the men are Irish and gentlemen, the horses are English.'

They went on to Dettigen and Fontenoy where they found that on the other side there were often as many Irish as they had themselves. 'Sometimes,' wrote one, 'I feel it is some kind of

Civil disturbance we contend.' They kept their humour, too, with them and the colour bearer, Cornet Richardson, who 'received seven and thirty cuts and shots upon his body and through his clothes, besides many of the standard, and being questioned how he contrived to save the Colours, he observed, that if the wood of the standard had not been made of iron it would have been cut in two'. When the regiment lined up at Fontenoy they found that not only were they fully complemented but that they had one man too many. He was ordered to be kept 'at his own expense' until a vacancy occurred!

The Black Horse was little different from any of the other regiments in that they collected a great deal of lore around them, but somehow it always seemed to have a more dramatic touch with this regiment. One of their soldiers had his horse shot from under him at Fontenoy, and wasn't seen until the next day when the regiments assembled again. He was called to account for his movements but showing rightful indignation demanded a court martial. At this he brought forward a Welsh officer who testified that the Irishman called on them in the battle to be allowed to march with them as his horse had been shot. Then to prove that he was worth a place with the Welsh Fusiliers he 'behaved with uncommon intrepidity and conduct'. The cavalryman was restored to his troop with honour and the commanding officer promoted him to the rank of lieutenant.

But probably one of the strangest stories is told about the regiment's quartermaster Jackson, the son of another quartermaster of the regiment. Jackson junior went to sea but in a foray into Spain was captured by the Spaniards who were in turn attacked by the Moors – and Jackson became their prisoner. Put up in Oran and offered as a slave he was bought in by the local British Consul and after a few years working with the family he arrived back in Ireland where his father resigned his warrant in favour of his son.

One day some years later, Jackson was passing through the gates of Dublin Castle and was surprised as a sentry on duty concealed his face as he went by. He couldn't put the incident out of his mind and watched out for another occasion when the same man was there. When he approached the sentry Jackson was astounded to find that it was the Consul of Oran – the man who had bought him out of slavery! The story he told was that shortly after Jackson's departure he had overrun his allowance and falling upon hard times had enlisted with the first recruiting sergeant he met on arrival in England. Jackson obtained the former Consul's discharge from the infantry and had him appointed a trooper with the Black Horse, where he could keep an eye on him. But within six months 'the unfortunate Consul died of brandy and a broken heart'.

It is hard to believe the claim of the writer in the *Dublin Penny Journal* that the regiment returned from the war 'there never having been an instance of a man having deserted – there was never a man or horse belonging to it taken by the enemy nor a man tried by a general court martial – there was but six men died who died a natural death; and there were thirty-seven private men promoted to commission'.

This regiment was just one of four regiments of horse in Ireland in the eighteenth century. All were raised originally in England but eventually came to place a great amount of attention on recruiting in Ireland. One man enlisted and lived to regret the day – eventually putting his feelings into a ballad:

> '*I lived as happy as a prince when I was in the North,*
> *And the first of my misfortunes was to list in the Black Horse.*'

The regiments took their nicknames from facings on their red uniforms. The Fourth was Black; the First was the Blue Horse; the Second was the Green Horse; but seldom did anyone affix a like nickname to the Third – their facings were yellow.

Life for the Four Regiments of Horse was comparatively easy in Ireland; there was really little fighting to be done and anyway the cavalrymen considered themselves a cut above ordinary soldiers. But when they stepped outside Ireland the going became tougher; yet they generally managed to retain the old reputation as fighting men. At Balaclava, where one of the Inniskilling regiments played its part in the Heavy Brigade, there was Lord Lucan and Captain Nolan allowing an age-old dispute between the two of them to get in the way of orders, causing in the end the disastrous reversal that the Light Brigade suffered in the historic charge. Only two Irishmen could have let their personal feud take precedence over that between Russia and Britain.

But somehow it has always been a matter of personalities where the Irish are concerned. The three Napier brothers, brilliant historians, tacticians and soldiers, won fame for themselves far away from the small village of Celbridge where they were born. The three brothers took part in Moore's retreat to Corunna in the winter of 1808–9, Charles being left with four soldiers in the extreme front when their regiment was recalled. Immediately surrounded, Napier saw the four soldiers bayoneted to death. Then he was struck down and stabbed and clubbed repeatedly. But a French drummer stepped in and saved him, eventually helping Napier back along the lines. Suddenly they were confronted by a lone soldier in the uniform of Napier's regiment. 'The soldier,' wrote Napier,

> instantly halted, recovered his arms, and cocked his piece, looking fiercely at us to make out the situation. Then he levelled at my French drummer; but I struck up his musket calling out, 'For God's sake don't fire! I am a prisoner, badly wounded, and can't help you; surrender.' 'For why would I surrender?' the soldier shouted in the deepest of Irish brogues. 'Because', said I, 'there are at least twenty

At Aughrim in the west of Ireland in 1691 was fought the last battle between the forces of King James II and King William III – the two deadly enemies whose deeds still cause more than a muttering of anger among the Irish.

The Connaught Rangers at the storming of 'the impenetrable' Cuidad Rodrigo, 1812. Wellington's orders had been: 'The place must be stormed.' It was – by the fierce fighting Rangers. It wasn't too long before the British had forgotten the great deeds of the Regiment . . . .

'acing page 80]

Ned Kelly, pictured just before his execution at the age of 24. As the white execution mask was slipped over his head Kelly sighed: 'Such is life.' And few characters led such a life of violence in Australia.

The Kelly Gang was certainly 'Wanted' – this was the ultimate reward – a fantastic £8,000 – which was offered for their capture in 1879. It is believed to be, comparatively, the greatest reward offered for a criminal anywhere.

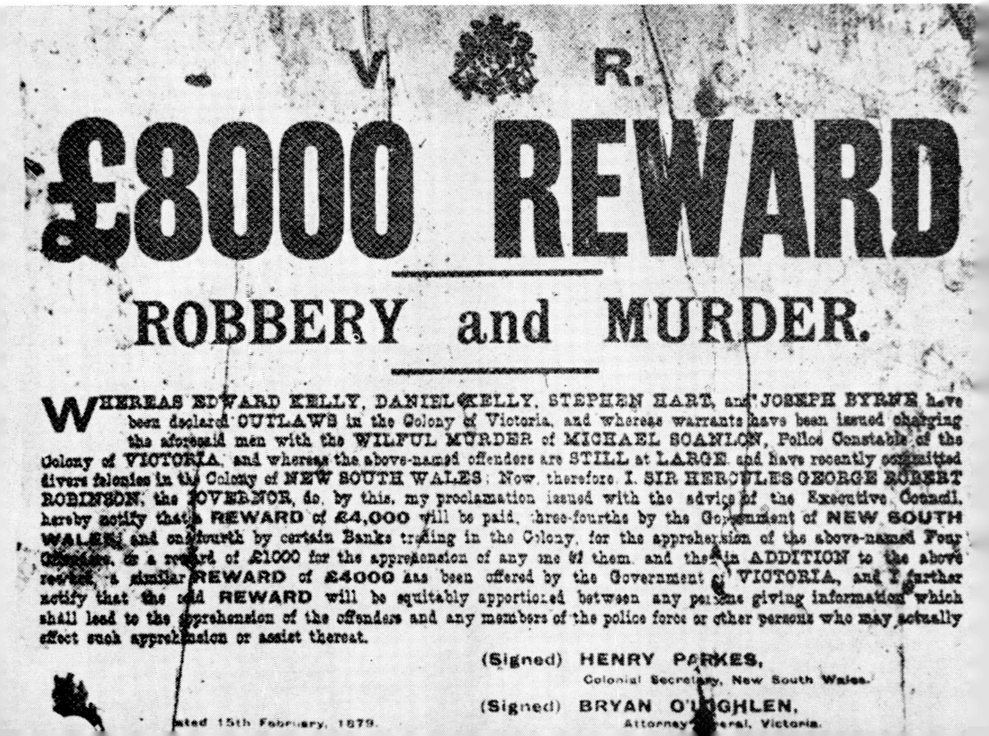

V. R.

£8000 REWARD

ROBBERY and MURDER.

WHEREAS EDWARD KELLY, DANIEL KELLY, STEPHEN HART, and JOSEPH BYRNE have been declared OUTLAWS in the Colony of Victoria, and whereas warrants have been issued charging the aforesaid men with the WILFUL MURDER of MICHAEL SCANLON, Police Constable of the Colony of VICTORIA, and whereas the above-named offenders are STILL at LARGE and have recently committed divers felonies in the Colony of NEW SOUTH WALES: Now, therefore, I, SIR HERCULES GEORGE ROBERT ROBINSON, the GOVERNOR, do, by this, my proclamation issued with the advice of the Executive Council, hereby notify that a REWARD of £4,000 will be paid, three-fourths by the Government of NEW SOUTH WALES and one-fourth by certain Banks trading in the Colony, for the apprehension of the above-named Four Offenders, or a reward of £1000 for the apprehension of any one of them, and that in ADDITION to the above reward, a similar REWARD of £4000 has been offered by the Government of VICTORIA, and I further notify that the said REWARD will be equitably apportioned between any persons giving information which shall lead to the apprehension of the offenders and any members of the police force or other persons who may actually effect such apprehension or assist thereat.

(Signed) HENRY PARKES,
Colonial Secretary, New South Wales.

(Signed) BRYAN O'LOGHLEN,
Attorney-General, Victoria.

Dated 15th February, 1879.

> men upon you.' 'Well if I must surrender, there!' he exclaimed, dashing down his firelock across their legs and making them jump – 'there's me firelock for yez'. Then coming close up, he threw his arm around me, and giving the drummer a push that sent him and one or two more reeling against a wall he shouted out, 'Stand back, ye bloody spalpeens! – I'll carry him meself. Bad luck to the whole of yez!

The Napier story continued with an astounding career. Not only did he get home after Corunna – more than many an Irishman, including General Moore – but he lived through some amazing encounters. While on Wellington's staff he was shot through the face. 'My jaws are crooked,' he wrote after hospital in Lisbon 'and will always be so; my mouth opens but stiffly.' He could not be kept away from the action. He was going back to the front when he heard the noise of a battle and approached some soldiers carrying a litter covered with a blanket. 'What officer is that?' he asked.

'Captain Napier, of the 32nd. A broken limb,' came the reply.

Another stretcher party came up. 'Who is that,' he enquired.

'Captain Napier of the 43rd mortally wounded,' came the reply.

Charles Napier glanced briefly at his two brothers and went on to the front. The three of them returned – the 'mortally wounded' one deceived them all and lived. But from one battle they were able to account for twenty-three wounds between the three of them. The Napiers brought everything into war – courage, ability and a grand arrogance. Once, after causing great destruction during his conquest of Scinde, Charles Napier summoned Hyderabad to surrender. Asked for terms he offered 'life – and nothing else'. And he added that they would have to make their minds up in a matter of hours for by midday 'the dead will be buried and my soldiers will have had their breakfasts'.

The story of the Lawrence brothers – five of them gained distinction with the English armies – ranks with that of the Napiers. Sir Henry Lawrence's part in the story of the British Empire will probably be remembered longer than any of his brothers. He was in command of Lucknow in 1857 when he used a phrase that is very familiar to Irish lips. As he was struck down by an accidental explosion he called to his officers: 'No surrender!' Then with his dying words he called: 'Let every man die at his post, but never make terms. God help the women and children.' During his earlier defence of the area he had decided to pull back all his troops to Lucknow. This entailed blowing up a nearby fort and his message went out: 'Spike your guns well, blow up the fort and retire at midnight.' Exactly on midnight the regiment marched out of the fort to the Governor's residency without a casualty. When they were safely away there was a tremendous explosion, a fountain of fire leapt in the air and the fort was blown to smithereens. But somehow, somewhere there had to be an Irishman who was just out of step at the last minute – and sure enough there was. This one had been gloriously drunk when the regiment marched away. No one missed him, and when the blast went he went too. He awoke in the early dawn in the middle of a heap of rubble and not an idea of what had happened. Soon afterwards the sentries at the gates of Lucknow heard the pleading voice: 'Ah, begod, and why the devil won't ye open up the gate and let a Dublinman through!' When they did they found that the soldier had recovered well from the drink and the explosion and had had the foresight to harness a couple of bullocks to a wagon loaded with ammunition and was driving them into the city. Not a word is to be found of Lawrence's reaction!

India was a place that saw so many heroics on the part of

Irishmen fighting for the Crown that it has formed its own vital place in the concept of Irishmen in the service of the British. While great soldiers led and fought their way into history in the Punjab and Lucknow and in the Gurkha Wars, and carried England's name to glory, it was the insensitivity, the absolute lack of humanity on the part of the military caste that was to virtually bring to an end the great exodus of men who were willing to fight on England's side.

The terrible truth, that the English would never be able to understand the Irish, was bluntly brought home to Ireland in the years that led up to 1920. In 1916, the leaders of the revolution were shot in Dublin; in 1920, in a further effort to suppress the feelings of the Irish the Black and Tans, an undisciplined murderous force, were unleashed on Ireland by Lloyd George. There wasn't an Irishman anywhere who didn't know of the terror the Tans brought with them as they roved barbarously through the country – and this certainly included the thousands of Irishmen serving with the British forces. All through the First World War the Irish had rallied to the service of the crown; the Somme was littered with Irish bones; the list of VC's was distinguished by the Irish names. Some Irish politicians described service in the British Army as 'the path of honour for Irishmen'. The number that died for Britain went to the fifty thousand mark, and that from a land so long under the stern boot of England. There were some eighty battalions of Irish infantry alone in the Great War – Inniskillings, Munsters, Hussars, Dragoons, Lancers, Guards, and the battle-hardened Connaught Rangers brought the total of fighting Irishmen up to almost 400,000 from a population of four million.

The place of the Connaught Rangers in history was safe long before the great blot was to obscure just about everything that the men of the West had fought for. Badajoz, the Alma,

Gallipoli . . . their battle honours were long and renowned. Then in Jullundur, in the raging heat of June came – the last mutiny of the British Army.

Astounded and disgusted by news of the brutalities being meted out to their friends and relatives at home, 'C' Company of the Rangers were so incensed that they refused point blank to carry out any more orders issued by anyone connected with the British Army. They were soon joined by others, and it became evident that their nickname 'the Devil's Own' had another side to it. Stubbornness was allied to their known courage. All efforts to talk the continually growing group of mutineers into giving up 'their silly act' only intensified their feelings. They held a meeting and it was left open to any man among them to join the mutineers or not. Only some twenty men decided to opt out and no hostility was shown to these. A committee was selected; the Union Jack at Jullundur was replaced by the Irish tricolour, stitched together by men who had bought lengths of material from the local bazaars. The four hundred men of the Rangers, their average age twenty-two, continued their mutiny. They mounted sentry and did all that was required to keep their own position intact. They continually repeated their reasons for the mutiny to their officers. When terms of surrender were eventually reached, the Rangers were marched to 'a new camp' outside the cantonment on the plain. Here they were subjected to the greatest of inhumanities – threatened with death by a squad of fully-armed troops and only saved by the intervention of a priest. They were made to live under canvas, something no British troops were ever expected to do in the broiling heat of India, they received little rations or medical supplies, and even this treatment was nothing compared with the dreadful hardships of men bound with leg irons and getting nothing more than black bread and weak tea for food. News of the mutiny

PART 2

America, Even Bigger

> meeting the dauntless Irish troops who opposed them in the last great push . . . the Irishmen had endured such constant attacks that it was thought that they must be utterly demoralised, but always they seemed to find a new energy with which to fight their assailants, and in the end the flower of the German Army withered and faded away as an effective force.

But, as has so often been proved in war, the friends of today can be the enemies of tomorrow. No one, it seems, keeps a credit and debit side in the ledger of heroics, courage and bravery.

It was from the 1920s onwards that Ireland's part in the British Army scene decreased. But again when war faced the old adversary there were hundreds of thousands of Irishmen involved, willing to take on Hitler, Mussolini or anyone else threatening Britain. And when the final surrender came the greatest hero of the war, Montgomery, the man from County Donegal, was there to accept it from the Germans.

And no doubt if there was a war tomorrow the exodus would be just as great to stand by England's side, which just adds to Britain's dilemma: Who can understand the Irish?

spread to Solan where other companies of the Rangers were stationed, and it was here that one man stepped forward and calling out his name and number identified himself as the leader. When eventually the mutiny was put down and the long months of terrible hardship endured, those words of Private James Daly were well remembered. He was one of fourteen men sentenced to death for their part in the mutiny; when the sentences were reviewed Daly's was the only one left standing.

T P Kilfeather in his detailed book, *The Connaught Rangers*, begins his story at this point:

> It was ordered by Major-General Sir G. de S. Barrow, K.C.B., K.C.M.G. of northern command of the British Army in India, from his headquarters at Murree, that at six o'clock precisely on the morning of 2 November, 1920, Private James Joseph Daly, age 22 years, of the 1st battalion The Connaught Rangers, regimental number 35025, from Tyrrellpass, county Westmeath, Ireland, would be executed by a firing party at Dagshai prison.

The final act of the drama that began on that hot day in June now moved inexorably towards its conclusion. Daly, from a family all of whom had served with the British army, would get no reprieve. The full harrowing details of the final minutes of this young soldier's life were written down by Father G B Baker, the priest who had stopped the wholesale slaughter of the company during the height of the mutiny.

When Father Baker went to the cell on the morning of the execution he saw Daly standing 'pale, somewhat thin and unwashed, and his clothes so old and dirty'. The clothes of the soldier, the priest was told, had not been washed or changed since that day of surrender in July. The priest took his place behind the prisoner and they marched out. When they stopped the provost sergeant produced a long, black serge bag which he tried to put over the soldier's head. But he shook it off saying, 'I don't want this, I want to die like an Irishman.' The priest records that there was then a scuffle and seeing trouble ahead he stepped forward and coaxed Daly to put on the bag 'both for his own sake and the sake of the firing party'. Before doing so he begged permission to see his friends. But no permission was given and the soldier was guided to a leaden chair where he asked, 'Is this where they are going to shoot me?' Then he lifted the bag off his head again and there was a rush at him but he told them calmly that he only wanted a look around. Again he asked the priest that he be allowed to see his friends and one in particular for the last time, but no one could help. He fought off efforts to tie him down, won his last battle—and then came the volley of death.

It was without a doubt one of the saddest, stupidest episodes in the whole history not only of a great regiment but also in the history of Britain's relations with the Irishmen who opted to fight with her. The strain of the news from home, the ineptitude of the officers dealing with the situation, heralded another great split between Britain and Ireland. Might Private Daly not have been set free considering all that the British owed the Irish? Were memories so short as to forget the first World War when General Foch said of the Irish with the British 'that never once did they the Irish fail me in those terrible days . . . they gave their lives freely'? Foch in his tribute went on to emphasise their record of courage:

> I know of no better tribute to Irish valour than that paid after the armistice by one of the German High Command, whom I had known in happier days. I asked him if he could tell me when he had first noted the declining morale of his own troops, and he replied that it was after the picked troops under his command had had repeated experience of

CHAPTER I

A Sort of Tir-na-nOg

THERE IS AN old legend that somewhere off the west coast of Ireland lies Tir-na-nOg – the Land of Youth, where the sun always shines, where the girls are beautiful and where a man may live in blissful ignorance of the world's mad capers. Maybe the Irish were hoping to land there when they set sail westwards . . . but they found America instead. And when the first Irishmen returned they brought back tales of a real wonderland, a wonderland that may have stirred Columbus to set out and see if these weren't just wild Irish stories. When it was confirmed that there was a land, not quite Tir-na-nOg, but near enough to it to make a man happy, the Irish set out in droves. They founded Boston (and still hold it), Pennsylvania, Baltimore, Salem, Carrolltown, Palmer, Worcester, Maine and they set up their own mighty colonies in New York and Philadelphia. They found that the world might be a big place but America was even bigger. In the beginning the exodus was merely a trickle, then in the time of Cromwell it became a flood. If the Irish were lucky they got out on an emigrant ship – if they were unlucky they were shipped off in slave boats. One slave trader, Captain John Vernon from Bristol, supplied 250 women between the ages of fourteen and forty from Wexford, Waterford and Cork, to points west, many of them becoming mistresses of the Puritan planters.

The emigrants landed and farmed and traded and mixed with other races – and when the opportunity came they fought. There hasn't been a fight in the United States worthy of the name that hasn't had an Irishman somewhere in the middle of it. From Davy Crockett at the Alamo to Billy the Kid in Lincoln County; from the battle of Bunker Hill with Washington to the square ring at Madison Gardens; from the Federals at Bull Run to the Confederates at the same place – the Irish were never out of it.

Some people find it hard at first glance to understand why the British ever lost America in the War of Independence. Even Washington himself expressed surprise at the fact that he ever won – in his estimation the whole affair had all the marks of fiction. Yet the answer was there all time – the Irish backlash. There was the great background of Irish hatred for Colonial rule; a hatred that no amount of cannon, men or money could hope to beat off. When the British had surrendered, Lord Mountjoy said: 'England has lost America through the exertions of Irish immigrants.'

So Hibernian was the revolutionary army that in June 1775 over seventy per cent of Washington's land forces and fifty per cent of his navy were Irish; at the end of the war in 1782 this number had increased by ten per cent in the army and five per cent in the navy. The 'Pennsylvania Line', probably the most famous corp in the revolutionary army was renamed 'The Line to Ireland' because of its solid Irish membership, and General Harry Lee, who gave them the name, said of them: 'Bold and daring they (the Irish) are impatient and refractory and would always prefer an appeal to the bayonet to a toilsome march.'

The very first scrap in the revolution was led by an Irishman – Major General John Sullivan – when he stormed Fort William and Mary and got away with the guns that were to arm the men who fought on Bunker Hill. This was the point at which British hold on America slipped loose. All around the Colonists, men were marching and drilling, guns and powder were being hidden away for the day . . . and then came Sullivan's horde of rifles from the Fort.

Five hundred and fifty yards from Boston was the twin settlement of Charlestown, and behind this town were three hills – one of them, Bunker Hill, was destined to become a focal point of world history, the other two were Breed's Hill and Morton's Hill.

The leading militant Massachusetts leaders, John Hancock and Samuel Adams, were out of the area at a congress when the first moves were made, and the leadership fell to Doctor Joseph Warren, a native of Ireland, and three others – General Artemas Ward, Israel Putnam and John Stark.

The leaders of the Revolution knew well that their men were ill-equipped against the British, they were badly trained when compared to the Colonists – and for what was going to be a war they had a mere six cannon. But they knew well that they had an abundant store of Irish resentment behind them. Four hours of digging on a June night in 1775 saw the completion of one of the best defences built against war – it was a shoulder-high earthen fort, capable of holding off rifle and long-range cannon. The British had not a clue of what was going on – until the morning when they were confounded by the fort that had appeared above Charlestown. They tried to blow it away by gunfire from their warships in the bay below – but the cannon balls just bounced off the defences. The bombardment became so great that the forces in the fort began to waver . . . but they stayed put. Eventually the British decided that the only way to take the encampment was to land detachments of their best troops at the foot of the hills. Now faced with the long line of redcoats preparing to attack there was a new drop in morale. But Warren came to the rescue, he knew his countrymen well; knew that most of Stark's Hampshire Regiment were Irish and the best disciplined group on the hill; he knew too that one brave man can convert a hundred. He approached General Prescott who was commander-in-chief of the operation and to his surprise Prescott offered to serve under him. But Warren would not have it: he had come for his musket to fight as a private. His move provided the encouragement the garrison needed.

The British attacks were fierce and strong but the discipline of the men behind the barricades was unyielding. Whenever the British reached a point within powder range the rebel guns opened up. The slaughter was staggering, and each time the British moved they got the same answer from behind the barricades. But human endurance was one thing – lack of shot and powder was another. Supplies were running out for the men on the hills. Suddenly all resistance stopped and with a roar of victory the British soldiers rushed over the banks of their own dead with bayonets ready. Warren gathered a handful of men around him and formed a rearguard to allow time for most of the Americans to escape. One shot dropped him dead. The rebels were routed – but the British could not follow up with the *coup de grâce*, they were too tired, the ground was too rough and the sacrifice they had made on Bunker Hill was too great. The British casualties were almost half their force – 226 soldiers killed and 828 wounded, and 27 officers killed and 63 wounded. The American casualties were less than half this number, a point they never forgot. They may have been beaten in the battle but it was the starting point to winning the war.

Immediately after Charlestown and Bunker Hill new American army appointments were made: John Sullivan took command of the army besieging Boston; Colonels Ed Hand and William Irvine were given command of the Pennsylvania Regiment; Colonels John Fitzgerald and Stephen Moylan joined Washington as aides-de-camp. But one of the most memorable appointments in this all-Irish list was that of County Donegal-born Richard Montgomery.

Before he found himself on the American side Montgomery's life had been eventful enough for any man. He joined the English army and fought in Canada where he took part under Major General James Wolfe in capturing Quebec from the French. In this battle Wolfe had been defeated once, then climbed the cliffs at night and, just when victory was at hand, he was mortally wounded while his antagonist, Montcalm, lay dying too. Montgomery, upset by the death of his general, resigned his commission and settled in America where on the outbreak of war he was welcomed into the Revolutionary ranks. But a strange quirk of fate was awaiting Montgomery. He was given command of the army which Washington wanted to invade Canada. It was a small army but Montgomery battled on against tremendous odds, winning battle after battle. Eventually he faced Quebec and, rushing forward with the first group of his men, he was shot at point blank range. His troops fled and all night Montgomery's body lay on the freezing plains of Abraham where both Wolfe and Montcalm had met their death. When his body was found the next day it was frozen stiff – with his sword gripped in the dead hand pointing towards Quebec.

A year after the first shots in the War of Revolution the army found the generals from Ireland leading them into a whole string of victorious battles – at Long Island, Brandywine, Germantown and many other places. It would be hard to pick out the heroes from the fifteen hundred officers and twelve thousand men in the army who were unquestionably Irish. Washington realised full well the value of the Irish and he made 'St Patrick' the watchword on 17th March 1776 when the rebel forces broke into Boston after besieging it for eight months. The Irish returned the compliment when they made Washington a member of the Friendly Sons of St Patrick in New York. He wrote to them: 'I accept with singular pleasure the Ensign of so worthy a fraternity as that of the Sons of St Patrick in this city – a Society distinguished for the firm adherence of its members to the glorious cause in which we are embarked.'

The glorious cause was backed all the way by the Irish – even to the bank. When fortunes were pretty low in the Revolution a group from Philadelphia donated £300,000 to funds – a third of this coming from the Irish.

Peace came in 1783, but it wasn't the Utopia the Irish dreamed of; it wasn't their Tir-na-nOg, and could not be so long as they had their memories and word still came through of troubled times in their own land. At home United Irelanders were having it as tough as any group of insurgents and then Robert Emmet their leader was executed. The Irish in America demanded revenge. But America wasn't being talked into another war – at least she hoped not. But behind the country's back the Irish tempers still bubbled. Then came a chance in 1812 and a war began that has been called a dirty little war – an encounter that did no one any good.

It was rumoured that the British were searching American ships; an ultimatum was presented to London but it was not acknowledged. America declared war on Britain. It has been suggested that in fact the ship searching was only an excuse and that the Irish had been looking for something to give them a chance to have another crack at the English. This was it, and to show their appreciation they made up seventy per cent of the American army and sixty per cent of the navy. While not many

POBLACHT NA H EIREANN.

THE PROVISIONAL GOVERNMENT
OF THE
IRISH REPUBLIC
TO THE PEOPLE OF IRELAND.

IRISHMEN AND IRISHWOMEN: In the name of God and of the dead generations from which she receives her old tradition of nationhood, Ireland, through us, summons her children to her flag and strikes for her freedom.

Having organised and trained her manhood through her secret revolutionary organisation, the Irish Republican Brotherhood, and through her open military organisations, the Irish Volunteers and the Irish Citizen Army, having patiently perfected her discipline, having resolutely waited for the right moment to reveal itself, she now seizes that moment, and, supported by her exiled children in America and by gallant allies in Europe, but relying in the first on her own strength, she strikes in full confidence of victory.

We declare the right of the people of Ireland to the ownership of Ireland, and to the unfettered control of Irish destinies, to be sovereign and indefeasible. The long usurpation of that right by a foreign people and government has not extinguished the right, nor can it ever be extinguished except by the destruction of the Irish people. In every generation the Irish people have asserted their right to national freedom and sovereignty: six times during the past three hundred years they have asserted it in arms. Standing on that fundamental right and again asserting it in arms in the face of the world, we hereby proclaim the Irish Republic as a Sovereign Independent State, and we pledge our lives and the lives of our comrades-in-arms to the cause of its freedom, of its welfare, and of its exaltation among the nations.

The Irish Republic is entitled to, and hereby claims, the allegiance of every Irishman and Irishwoman. The Republic guarantees religious and civil liberty, equal rights and equal opportunities to all its citizens, and declares its resolve to pursue the happiness and prosperity of the whole nation and of all its parts, cherishing all the children of the nation equally, and oblivious of the differences carefully fostered by an alien government, which have divided a minority from the majority in the past.

Until our arms have brought the opportune moment for the establishment of a permanent National Government, representative of the whole people of Ireland and elected by the suffrages of all her men and women, the Provisional Government, hereby constituted, will administer the civil and military affairs of the Republic in trust for the people.

We place the cause of the Irish Republic under the protection of the Most High God, Whose blessing we invoke upon our arms, and we pray that no one who serves that cause will dishonour it by cowardice, inhumanity, or rapine. In this supreme hour the Irish nation must, by its valour and discipline and by the readiness of its children to sacrifice themselves for the common good, prove itself worthy of the august destiny to which it is called.

Signed on Behalf of the Provisional Government,

THOMAS J. CLARKE,
SEAN Mac DIARMADA, THOMAS MacDONAGH,
P. H. PEARSE, EAMONN CEANNT,
JAMES CONNOLLY, JOSEPH PLUNKETT

A facsimile reproduction of the Republican Proclamation issued on Easter Monday, 1916

Republican Proclamation issued on Easter Monday, 1916. The seven signatories were later executed.

Facing page 96]

Unique photograph of Sackville Street in flames during the Irish rebellion – May 1916.

A rare photograph of two of the armed rebels taken in 1916 during the Easter Uprising.

[*Facing page*

battles were won, all of the encounters on field and sea were stubbornly contested. General Ripley, as Irish as any, won Chippewa; Major MacNeil was commended by Washington for the way in which he headed three charges of the 11th Regiment in the same battle. The Carrolls, Millers and MacDonoughs were in just about every battle while the Coffees played a big part.

So famous did the name Coffee become that no history of Tennessee or Kentucky would be complete without a mention of Coffee's Scouts. This was a regiment of cavalry raised by 'brave Jack Coffee' from among the backwoodsmen of those two regions. Wherever they went Coffee's Scouts brought pleasure to Americans and fear to the enemy.

Out of the war came one big victory – that won by a son of Irish immigrants, Andrew Jackson. Jackson commanded New Orleans where his second-in-command was another Irishman, General William Carroll; and in the ranks was a soldier, the son of Irish parents, whose name was to become part of the great folk legend of the time – Davy Crockett. Beside these there was Coffee and his three thousand men, as well as some two thousand men from Kentucky, mostly Irish or of Irish extraction, all moving to New Orleans to face up to one of the strongest British forces ever assembled against America. The British crowded the seas with a great and heavily laden fleet, and their army and navy should have had no trouble in wiping out the Americans.

While New Orleans waited with apprehension for the expected full-scale attack, Andrew Jackson took over. He was fresh from successful campaigns against the Indians and the Spanish at Florida. He was told to hold New Orleans at all costs. At first this must have seemed a monumental task but with the irregular forces from Kentucky and Tennessee, urged on by Jack Coffee and General Carroll, the situation was not lost. Jackson, according to contemporary accounts, was

> a tall gaunt man, of very erect carriage, with a countenance full of stern decision and fearless energy, but furrowed with care and anxiety. His complexion was sallow and unhealthy, his hair was iron grey, and his body thin and emaciated, like that of one who had just recovered from a lingering and painful illness. But the fierce glare of his bright and hawk-like eyes betrayed a soul and spirit which triumphed over all the infirmities of the body. His dress was simple and nearly threadbare. A small leather cap protected his head, and a short Spanish blue cloak his body, whilst his feet and legs were encased in high dragoon boots, long ignorant of polish or blacking, which reached to his knees. In age he appeared to have passed about forty-five winters.

Little doubt from that description why he earned the name of 'Hickory'.

In New Orleans he had to contend with treason and disaster . . . rumours that became more frequent when the British navy made short work of the small American force of gunboats. The invading army was fully landed on 21st December 1814 complete with rockets, field guns and a great array of artillery. Waiting the attack the American soldiers had a collection of small cannon, muskets, rifles and 'so great was the lack of war munitions that even the flints of the privateers' rifles were received as a precious prize and were forthwith fitted to muskets'.

The British sent in their first detachment of troops but Jackson, who had just received two American battleships, the *Carolina* and the *Louisiana*, sent these down river where they effectively blasted the British soldiers. There were many skirmishes in the next few days as the British were held under fire, but eventually in another river battle the *Carolina* was raked with British guns and blew up; the *Louisiana* got away. Seven days after the first march the British soldiers began to move from this besieged position. On the foggy morning of 1st January 1815 they were only four hundred yards from Jackson's lines. When the mist lifted the American camp lay completely exposed; soldiers were parading, flags were flying, bands playing. Suddenly the British guns opened up and a scene of absolute panic met the gunners' gaze – but it was only for an instant. Quickly the soldiers, the backwoodsmen, the pioneers, took up positions and soon it was a two-way roar of cannon. Heavy as the invading force of guns was they seemed to have little effect on the defences which Jackson had supervised, while the American guns, strategically placed, soon had the whole affair well under control.

Leading the British was Lord Pakenham. He tried ploy after ploy and in ordinary circumstances these would surely have worked, but against the old campaigners of Indian sieges and men with a national debt to repay he was lost. Pakenham led his men time after time against the well-entrenched defenders; eventually he was hit and died in the arms of his aide-de-camp. When the battle ended in victory for Jackson, the British had suffered the incredible loss of two generals and fifteen hundred officers and men against the American loss of eight dead and fourteen wounded. The horror of the situation was that almost a fortnight before the fatal battle the Treaty of Ghent had been signed to end all hostilities between Britain and America, but there was no way other than the slow sea-crossing to send the message.

Jackson had won a notable victory; he went on to win more and become the seventh President of the United States, just one of the many with Northern Irish blood who became Presidents of the United States. As for the others, most of them headed back to the life Jackson himself had once lived: to log cabins, built by themselves for their own little groups, with the spirit to fight a living from the land. There were some who, like Davy Crockett, didn't get back to a peaceful life. Possibly Crockett would not have been allowed to settle for he was a legendary figure even then with coonskin cap, buckskin hunting shirt and fringed leggings. In fact if Davy Crockett hadn't been born to his Northern Ireland parents, history would have had to invent him. He was one of the most remarkable hunters of all time in America and with his trusty rifle 'Betsy' he was credited with killing 107 bears. He was a magnificent shot, a superb scout and a man who lived up to his motto: 'Be sure it's right then go right ahead.' He was elected to the Tennessee legislature and had an illustrious political career which ended with election to Congress in 1827. He lost his seat in 1835 when he took a stand against his old boss, Andrew Jackson. Then once again he shouldered his old 'Betsy' and headed off in search of a good war to fight. He found it at the Alamo where a bloody war between Texas and Mexico was being fought. He joined the Texans and was one of a small handful of defenders left in the Fort when it was taken by the Mexicans under Santa-Anna. He fought fanatically and was one of the last to be killed 'without a groan, with a smile of scorn on his lips' and a dozen Mexican swords hacking him. That night the bodies of the defenders were heaped and burned . . . a dreadful ending to the Crockett legend.

No doubt when the full-scale war between the United States and Mexico got under way in 1846 there were many who remembered the callous treatment meted out to the men of the Alamo. Over half the American army was claimed to be Irish – certainly there was one corp of two thousand native-born Irish in the field. And they were led by General 'Old Rough and Ready' Zachary Taylor, an Irishman, helped by General W Butler, Colonel Pierce Butler, General Burke and a barrage of

Burkes, O'Briens and Murphys. Taylor, an old battler by this time, rode his white horse to victory against Santa-Anna – at a loss that had him writing afterwards, 'I have no exultation in our success when I miss all the familiar faces.' Major Theodore O'Hara, an Irish veteran of the war, put it another way in his poem 'Bivouac of the Dead':

On Fate's eternal camping ground
Their silent tents are spread,
And glory guards with column round
The bivouacs of the dead.

The heroes of the Mexican war on the American side provide a list that is ninety per cent Irish. Under Taylor at Buena Vista a section of the artillery commanded by Lieutenant Paul O'Brien was cut off from the main part of the force. Under heavy attack O'Brien stuck to his post, saw some of his soldiers running and his guns captured, but with rifle fire he held off the Mexicans until help came. His guns were recaptured and stand in glory at West Point today. Another hero was General James Shiels, a native of Dungannon who fought, although wounded, some of the gamest battles of the war. But Shiels left behind him another mark in the book of history – he once challenged Lincoln to a duel. He handed out the challenge after Lincoln had accepted responsibility for a series of articles written by his fiancée, Mary Todd, and her friend, Julia Jayne, in a newspaper. The articles sneered at Shiels's rustic manners and at the mere fact that he was an Irishman. Lincoln chose broadswords as the fighting weapon and the two met in an isolated Missouri sand bar. But while they were waiting for the seconds to arrange details the two men got talking, and became friends, a friendship that lasted through life. Eventually Lincoln apologised in public for the articles.

Just as the Irish fought on both sides of Europe's war, they were to be found on both sides in America – fighting for her and also for the Mexican side. One who achieved notoriety was John Riley and he commanded Mexico's San Patricio Battalion. Born in Ireland in 1817 he had been a private in the British Army, then joined the American forces and was with Taylor when the Mexican campaign started. The day before hostilities began he asked for permission to go to Mass. This was granted and he disappeared – for a while. Eventually he was found again, second-in-command of the San Patricio Battalion, a group of foreigners who fought long and hard against the Americans.

Riley was captured by Shiels and out of the seventy or so men who survived in the battalion twenty-seven were natives of Ireland. A military court assembled immediately the men were captured and with frightening speed forty-nine men were sentenced to be hanged on the spot – mostly because they had deserted the American forces. Of those hanged seventeen were Irish. Riley escaped, because he had technically deserted before war had begun. He was sentenced to fifty lashes of a rawhide whip and the letter 'D' for deserter branded on his face. When the sentence was carried out Riley was drummed out of the service and returned to the Mexican army where he was promoted to Colonel.

It was, as one writer of the time, said 'not a great time to be a winner and a damn bad time to be a loser'. But through the winning and the losing the Irish survived four big American wars and lived on in a sort of peace . . .

CHAPTER 2

The 69th and Billy The Kid

WHY THE IRISH settled so happily in America is probably best summed up by the action of Jasper O'Farrell, a Dublinman born and bred. O'Farrell became a cavalryman during the Indian uprising in 1847 and among his war exploits was the capture of two beautiful Indian girls. No doubt there was great camp chat about O'Farrell's trophy but it wasn't long before he realised that life was hard enough without having to keep two women; to keep even one a man would need some sort of material backing. So the bold Jasper decided to begin at the beginning and at the first opportunity he did a swap with a German immigrant – trading the two Indian girls for a cow.

This was the great thing about America, it was a land where a man could trade; where he could own a cow and a horse and a house and the Government wouldn't slap a wanted notice on him and declare all his goods illegal; where if he worked well and fought well they might even name a street after him, as they eventually did in San Francisco in honour of the same Jasper O'Farrell.

Others went and struggled – not always with the same results. No matter how much heart you put into your efforts and no matter what the rewards there was still the memory of home.

One emigrant in the gold fields told how it really was when he wrote to an Irish newspaper in 1849:

> We are in a tent near San Francisco in a place called Happy Valley – something like Rush (a small Dublin holiday resort), but with no proper houses, streets or buildings, being mostly tents. San Francisco is about as big as Balbriggan. The harbour is full of ships lying idle, crews, captains and all hands having deserted and made off for the mines. I am here five weeks; I make about half an ounce of gold a day. It's hard digging, eight feet down and then three to the rock, sometimes deeper. There are thieves in plenty; the first time they are caught they are cow-hided or their ears are cut off; the second time they are either hanged or shot. Provisions are very costly; 3s for a loaf; 4s for an egg or an orange; 2s for a pound of sugar; 12s for a bottle of ale; this sheet of notepaper cost me a shilling.

Material gains were one thing, there was also the great matter of conscience, something that caused more head scratching among the Irish who landed in America than among any other immigrants. At first it was all right: the Revolution was simple enough – they took the guns to fight the British, it didn't matter really that there was a bitter anti-Catholic faction on the same side. But other wars presented a different problem: they were expected to fight on the side of Protestant America against Catholic Spain and Mexico. They salved their conscience by detailing the benefits that accrued from having a strong anti-British America, which was their best chance of eventually winning Ireland back as their homeland. Then came the Civil War with its North and South conflict. Which side to fight on? The South, and justify it with materialism – that the freeing of so many slaves would mean little work for the Irish? The South, and justify it with the ideal that they would not stand by and see any land that wanted its own way of life manacled to another? Yet how could they fight on the South side when they had fled their own land and its tyrannical booting down of the native classes? And what about the Abolitionists – largely led by Protestants, many of whom denounced both black slavery and 'Popery' in the same breath. Where then to turn? It was as great a dilemma as ever faced a man, but when the war really began the Irish were in there fighting – on both sides. Words could easily be used to justify either cause but the fighters on the Northern side had a special reason for a smile when the British began to back the Confederates – they felt then that their choice of camps had definitely been right.

Statistics of the war are very muddled. One historian says that there was something like 150,000 men of Irish birth engaged in in the war, and that they were fairly evenly divided between the two sides. But generally speaking, it was a case of what geography had put together history was pulling apart and, similarly, what history had pulled apart geography was putting together. Protestant from the North and Republican Catholic from the South – of Ireland this time – found themselves shoulder to shoulder in each army. And what an array of officers and men were thrown up by the war – a great majority of them with Irish blood. Ulysses Grant with the Federals – and a bevy of other generals and top-ranking officers on each side: Sheridan who won the Shenandoah Valley for the Federals; Meade, the Gettysburg leader and winner; Kearney, Corcoran, Sullivan, Croghan, Patterson and Meagher of the Sword. If the North boasted of this collection of Protestant and Catholic Irish, the South could do the same: Irish patriot John Mitchel lost two sons in the Confederate Army against his old friend Meagher; Finnegan and Cleburne were but two of the top generals who were Irish born on the South side. Cleburne from Cork left behind a story that is passed down as a legend of Tennessee. While galloping across the battlefield at Franklin he saw a young soldier struggling to walk, his feet bloody and bare. Jumping off his horse the general pulled off his boots and passed them to the soldier with the comment: 'You need them more than I do.' Then he mounted and rode off – to die in the same battle without his boots on.

On the Southern side, too, there were battalions of Irish soldiers, one group in particular – the Louisiana Irish – taking more than their reputations as fighters on to the battlefield. In *Battlefields of the South* written by 'an English combatant' the comment after one battle was: 'As the majority of (Major) Wheat's command were Louisiana Irish they robbed the dead of their whiskey and were in high spirits when ordered to assail Sherman and Keyes.' They created havoc among the Yankees – many of whom were also Irish.

In any account of the Irish part in the Civil War the encounters of the Irish Brigade loom largest. Call it the Irish Brigade or Meagher's Brigade or Meagher's Zouaves or the 69th – the name doesn't matter but the story does, for in any account of the Fighting Irish no matter what other stone must be stepped over because of the vastness of the subject, no one can overlook Meagher and his men. When the war began, Thomas Meagher was not long resident in America. He had been arrested in Ireland in 1848 for the part he played in the Young Ireland movement and was sentenced to deportation to Tasmania for treason. With him went Smith O'Brien, John Mitchel, Terence Bellew McManus, Patrick O'Donoghue, John Martin, Izod O'Doherty, John Boyle O'Reilly, and J K Casey – the most important group of Irishmen ever to be deported and a group of men sadly missed in their famine-torn land. But Meagher, Mitchel and others made their escape from Tasmania and were warmly greeted in America. Meagher became a well-known lecturer, started the *Irish News*, and when Civil War was mooted formed his own corps of Zouaves, gathered entirely from Ireland and dedicated to fight for the North. They fought and their story is one of tremendous verve, vitality, humanity and wit. Meagher's Zouaves became part of the Irish Brigade at Arlington Heights where they marched to Bull Run and eventually came under the direct order of General Sherman. Bull Run . . . the first engagement between the two factions . . . the first meeting of raw recruits and well loaded guns . . . the first taste of blood and sight of death. The 69th Irish Brigade fought more than its share at Bull Run and all the time there was Meagher to rally them on. When his horse was shot from under him his great voice roared, 'Keep at them boys – remember Fontenoy.' And they 'kept at them' but the battalion was severely hit mainly because their red uniforms made a good target for the Confederates. Their flag bearer was shot but another took over. He too was wounded: Captain D P Conyngham, who served with the Brigade and wrote its history, continued the story:

> a rebel tried to shoot him dead but he grappled with them, shot the rebel and captured a rebel colour. Eventually he was overpowered and the trophy taken from him, beside being taken prisoner with his own flag. But he had a concealed revolver and shot the two men in charge of him took a captain's sword and a prisoner, which he brought in with him. His name was John D Keeffe.

George Wilkes, who saw the battle wrote a full description of it in his paper, *The Spirit of the Times*, and commented: 'Most prominent among them (the 69th) was Meagher, the Irish orator, who frequently during the contest of that turbulent day, waved the green banner of his regiment up and down the hottest line of fire.' Other reports were in the same vein, while one Southern paper said: 'No Southerner but feels that the Sixty-Ninth maintained the old reputation of Irish valour – on the wrong side. All honour to the Sixty-Ninth, even in its errors.'

Errors nor not, the Irish Brigade went on to win many honours – at a terrible price – in the Civil War. Historians down through the years have tried to pull apart the reputation of many of Ireland's fighting brigades, claiming that they were always thrown into a battle only when the real fighting had been done and generally suspecting the assessment of even the men who were there, but the reputation of the Irish Brigade in America has lived through it all and any assessment will only lend authority to people like Captain Conyngham and other contemporary writers who travelled with the Irish and fought side by side with them.

At Fair Oaks, the enemy retired battered and bruised before the charge of the Irish – a battle in which they boasted before the assault, 'We've never run yet, and we're not going to do it now.' Just how they lived up to this boast is shown by the story of the drummer boy hero. George Funk was his name and, although only a boy, he was out skirmishing on his own. While one of the Federal regiments was retiring, George spotted a rebel sharpshooter rise from behind a tree and fire after them. George moved off, came up behind the rebel and took him prisoner. 'It was an amusing sight,' writes the recorder, 'to see the little lad manly marching at a charge-bayonet, escorting his big prisoner to the rear.'

In *Leaves from the Diary of an Army Surgeon*, Dr Thomas Ellis wrote:

> There was the Irish Brigade in all the glory of a fair, free fight. Other men go into fights finely, sternly or indifferently but the only man that really loves it, after all, is the green immortal Irishman. So there the brave lads from the old sod,

> with the chosen Meagher at their head, laughed, and fought, and joked as if it were the finest fun in the world. We saw one sitting on the edge of a ditch, wounded and perspiring in the hot sun with his feet in the water. As we rode by he called out to know if we had ever seen 'a boiled Irishman!'

But Fair Oaks wasn't all a joke – losses reported by Stonewall Jackson's Confederate forces numbered 6,738 and on the Federal side, 5,737.

And as the Brigade wove its way through the van of the fighting they collected more accolades like *The Times*'s comment of the soldiers who 'breathed fire and dirt'. They breathed it to immortality at the Battle of Antietam on 17th September 1862. Here under the command of General McClelland the Federals took on the Confederates under the renowned Robert E Lee. In the centre of the line the Irish faced the rebels who were firmly entrenched along a sunken road behind a breastwork of fences and rails. It all added up to a fierce artillery war, a war of assault and counterassault, and finally a massive hand-to-hand encounter. The Confederates behind their strongly entrenched positions beat back wave after wave of Union troops. Bloody Lane they called the position held by the Confederates – a name given as the number of dead piled up after each effort to take over from the rebels. Either the position was taken or the Federals lost the battle. McClelland ordered the Irish in. They were cut to ribbons but still they went on – eight men carried the green flag into the battle and died; finally it was waved under the nose of the enemy by Captain James McGee. Meagher had his horse shot from under him; the great heap of dead was added to; half a New York Regiment was wiped out in one volley; but the Irish kept on. 'Their cheers rose in one great surge of noise over the noise of the battle, over the roar of the multitude of artillery

. . .' wrote Doctor Ellis. 'Thus met, the rebel advance was checked and broken, and they were driven with awful slaughter.'

When McClelland saw the position was won he sent in another regiment to hold it and ordered the Irish to the rear. He was to report later: 'The Irish Brigade sustained its well earned reputation.' Over twenty thousand men died in that battle – and the loss to the Irish Brigade 'was out of proportion high'. The fearful picture of the battlefield that night should have been enough to send even the toughest-skinned soldier deserting. 'The mournful cry of the whip-poor-will, and the croaking of the frogs on the marshes, mingled with the groans of the dying and wounded, broke the solemn stillness that reigned over that field of carnage,' wrote Captain Conyngham, '. . . the dead lay piled about in all kinds of manner. Here are two men, a Federal and a rebel soldier with their bayonets driven through each other's breasts; both of them are dead and their features wear all the fierce expressions of the hate and passions of the conflict. Near them is a little drummer boy, of about fourteen; a piece of shell has gone through his drum and himself together. Poor child! he had beaten his last tattoo.'

But even in those fearful battle scenes at Fair Oaks and Antietam, Conyngham still saw the reason that justified Chesterton's line of 'all their wars are happy'.

A soldier whose cheek was laid open with a bullet, apologised to the surgeon who was dressing it. 'Sure doctor I wouldn't have come to you at all with this little scratch only the blood was blinding me and as soon as you have it all right I'll go back and have another slap at them rebels.'

Another Irishman brought in with a shattered arm asked the doctor: 'Is it bad?' When told that it would have to be amputated replied: 'You don't say, doctor, wasn't it lucky it wasn't my right arm?'

Led by Meagher the Brigade continued through the war and the two thousand men who survived Antietam went on to Fredericksburg where on a cold December day they fought as they had never fought before. Six times they assaulted an almost impregnable rebel position and six times they failed. When the count was taken, after the generals realised that no one could get it if the Irish failed, five regiments could only muster a mere two hundred men. Their bravery led the correspondent of the London *Times* to write:

> Never at Fontenoy, Albuere, or at Waterloo was more undaunted courage displayed by the sons of Erin than in those six frantic dashes which they delivered against the almost impregnable position of their foe . . . The bodies which lie in dense masses . . . are the best evidence of what manner of men they were who pressed on to death with the dauntlessness of a race which has gained glory on a thousand battlefields and never more richly deserved it than at the foot of Marye's Heights on the 13th day of December 1862.

It was a day that was never forgotten in America and one to recognise it was John F Kennedy when he came to Ireland in 1963 – he called it a day long-remembered in American history. 'At Fredericksburg, Virginia, thousands of men fought and died in one of the bloodiest battlefields of the American Civil War. One of the most brilliant stories of that day was written by a band of 1,200 men who went into battle wearing a green sprig in their hats.' He spoke about the battle, about Meagher and mentioned that even Robert E Lee had been overwhelmed by the Irish fight and that the Confederate general said: 'Never were men so brave . . . their brilliant, though hopeless, assaults on our lines, excited the hearty applause of our officers and soldiers.' President Kennedy unveiled a special treasure for the city of Dublin – one of the flags of the Fighting 69th. It carries the battle honours of Fredericksburg, Chancellorsville, Yorktown, Fair Oaks, Gaines Hill, Allen's Farm, Savage's Station, White Oak Bridge, Glendale, Malvern Hills, Antietam, Gettysburg, Bristoe's Station and others – each a chapter on its own. For each of these battles Meagher was there and in between times he was recruiting and recruiting. Going into one battle he had a hundred and twenty recruits who had signed up only the day previously. When the war ended the toll was high, but the battle had been won and the Brigade was disbanded.

It is possible in the saga of the Civil War to point to many other heroes but one should not be overlooked – Ulysses S Grant. In this general who led the Federal Army to its final victory, Irish blood flowed truly. He was the man of whom Lincoln said, 'He makes things git', and make things git he did, finishing off the long and bloody revolution.

If the Civil War and all it brought with it was not enough to place the Irish well and truly into the lore of the land there were other individuals willing and able to play their part. The Penns arrived from Cork to found Pennsylvania; the Starks, Whipples, Callalmores, Casses from Ulster strode into South Carolina and Alabama side by side with the O'Sullivans and Butlers and all became wealthy planters; Simon Kenton marched into a land that took part of his name – Kentucky; Patrick Calhoun left Ireland and fought some fantastic battles against the Red Indians as he pushed deep into the South Carolinas. His son, John Caldwell Calhoun, became vice-president of the United States. Sam Houston gave his sword and gun to Texas and was honoured with a town named after him, but not before he had lived with the Cherokee Indians for three years.

But in the early days the great trek West meant that the Irishman was more often fighting the Red Indians than living with them. The fights were brutal and decimating and it meant that the Irish soon became the best shots in the west. Two accounts come down of the ability of their shooting. In a local history of the New Hampshire towns of Derry and Londonderry the author, E L Parker, comments: 'Almost every soldier equalled William Tell as a marksman, and could aim his weapon at an opposer with as keen a relish. Those from the frontiers had gained this address against the savages and beasts of the forests.' Another writer, A G Bradley, described the guns carried by these early frontiersmen: 'Their rifles were inordinately long and heavy, bored out of solid iron for small bullets of sixty to the pound and carrying with precision up to eighty yards.' The Indians fought with a savage hatred of the pioneers and the Irish were the greatest sufferers. But somehow they managed to keep on going, eventually getting their groups settled down where they could defend themselves. One account of the methods used then tells of the men defending a fort against Indians and how two of them Grady and McQuiery, experienced Indian fighters, were battling in their bare feet against the Sioux. They had 'fixed shoestrings into loops to fit over the right foot and from thence to the trippers of their rifles – to kill themselves when all hope was lost. If the Indians passed over the barricades every man would stand erect, place the muzzle of his loaded rifle under his chin and take his own life rather than be captured and made to endure the inevitable torture.'

The Irish established themselves so well in the West that they could fight with the best – on the side of the law or against it. Mike Meagher was Marshal of Wichita and had Wyatt Earp serving under him; Miles Keogh, once a member of the Papal Guards at the Vatican died with other Irishmen in Custer's last stand; but probably the biggest single occurrence involving the Irish was the Lincoln County Cattle War in which the notorious

Billy The Kid played a central part. Henry McCarty was Billy's real name and his mother and father were Irish. The scrawny schoolboy they knew in Silver City grew up to be one of the most renowned legends of the West. He was running from the law for a long time before he got himself mixed up in the Lincoln Cattle War in New Mexico in 1878, but for some reason when he hit Lincoln City he seemed to have settled down. But trouble was only a quick draw away from anyone in a town like this where the Irish, made up of the Murphys and Rileys and Dolans, faced the Englishman Tunstall who had Alexander A McSween and other Irish on his side. Looking back on the war it seems that one side was just as unscrupulous as the other.

Billy was drawn into the fight when his boss Tunstall was murdered by the Murphy faction. Remorselessly he set about getting revenge, and again it was Irish blood after Irish blood. When two of the killers Baker and Morton surrendered after a fight Billy had them shot down in cold blood. The sheriff, whose name was Brady, was next. It looked as though Billy was heading for a complete clean-up. Efforts were made to talk him into giving up but they ended with a face-to-face confrontation across the one mud street of Lincoln.

On one side Murphy's store and directly opposite was the McSween bank and store. The Murphy faction surrounded the house and kept McSween, Billy The Kid and others under siege for three days. Then Murphy had the house set on fire and as the men ran out they were shot down. Last to leave was Billy the Kid; with six shooters blazing he stepped from the smoke and flames and shot dead two of the Murphy faction; then he escaped. He was captured, sentenced to hang – but, shooting down two guards, he got away again. Followed everywhere by Sheriff Garrett, once his friend, Billy eventually paid the debt. When

Garrett shot him Billy was only twenty-one. Murphy lived on in Lincoln. No one knows how many men died all because Irishmen and Englishmen let their old passions well up in the traditional hatred of each other and the traditional love of land.

'Go West young men' may have been a calling cry to pioneers then, it certainly was to the Irish and every road that leads west leads over a grave of a pioneer or soldier who took off hoping to find the land of eternal youth . . .

CHAPTER 3

South American Way

IF THE FIRST Irishman to land on foreign soil wasn't a priest he was likely to be a soldier, but it wasn't often that the unusual combination of student-priest turned mercenary cropped up. It did happen at Buenos Aires on the day Ambrose Higgins sailed in. He brought with him goods to sell from Spain and went on to become the most influential Irishman in the history of South America. Today they still sing legends in Peru and Chile to the memory of Higgins and his family. Not that he was alone there – the Murphys, O'Briens, O'Learys, Browns, Lynchs, Gallaghers, Mulhalls all made their mark down south and descendants of these first soldiers are still found in top positions in Brazil, Argentina and Chile today.

Most of the Irish moved to South America when the Spanish hold on that part of the world was wide and strong. They stayed on to become governors, commanders, leaders, generals and admirals, and one of their descendants Bernardo O'Higgins became the saviour of Chile. His story begins with Ambrose Higgins who arrived in Buenos Aires in the mid-eighteenth century. Ambrose, born in 1720 in either Meath or Sligo – there has always been disagreement as to his birthplace – found himself caught up in the great drift from the country while still in his teens. He went to Spain and studied for the priesthood, but finding it not to his liking he talked one of his relatives, who lived there, into financing his trip to South America. He landed in Buenos Aires with a collection of merchandise and quickly showed his salesmanship qualities; his next move took him to Lima – where he set up opposite the cathedral. If anyone could have seen the down-at-the-heel adventurer trying to sell his goods in one of the then poorer towns of South America, they could have been forgiven for writing him off as just another mad Irishman. But they reckoned without the special mixture of blarney and military ability that became very obvious as Higgins progressed through the land. His travels took him all over Peru and New Granada and with his golden tongue he made a fortune, enough indeed for him to offer his services to the Spanish Government in Chile. They took up his offer and, with the knowledge that the Irish could be quick with the sword as well as the tongue, sent Higgins off on a punitive expedition against the Araucanian Indians.

It was a late start in a military career, for Higgins was almost fifty at this time. But there was a shortage of good officers and the resourcefulness of the Irishman had won him many friends. He was commissioned Captain of Dragoons and set off on a military campaign that was long and arduous. The Araucanian Indians had been the terrors of the Spanish troops for years and consequently morale was very low. But Higgins saw that the Indians could be beaten at their own game. He formed a mounted force which was adept either as cavalry or infantry and soon had the upper hand. 'So judicious and rapid were his movements,' wrote Juan MacKenna, 'that he succeeded in surprising and attacking separately all the scattered troops of Araucanians, either killing or capturing them . . . after a bloody battle the Araucanian army abandoned the field to the enemy for the first time during the war.'

Although he won the battle, Higgins knew a lot had to be done to win over the Indians. He set to and showed that he had never lost his trading ability. Combining it and the discipline of a soldier's life he won over the Indians, to everyone's surprise. So successful was he that the Spaniards made him a Colonel, and quickly he leapfrogged up the promotion ladder. When he was sixty-six he was *mastre de campo* (or Commander-in-Chief) of the province of Concepción, the most important province in the country.

But Higgins still had a fear that because his name was so unfamiliar to the people he wasn't fully accepted. He had good reason for this – at times he had been called Ignes, Ihiggyns, Egis, and Higges – and he searched around for a title. One wasn't forthcoming from Spain – but Ireland proved a better hunting-ground. He discovered, through a nephew, that his family traced itself back to one Baron Ballinary. Before he could get the full documentation of his claim he was Governor and Captain General of Chile – to which the Spanish Government finally added the title of Baron of Ballinary. His full title now was Don Ambrosio O Higgins, Governor of Chile, El Baron Vallenar.

In between wars and peace pacts Ambrosio enjoyed himself. He was known as a very humane man and he fitted well into local politics and with the local people – so well in fact that one mistake almost marred his later life. He never showed any interest in marriage but stopped his career-bent energies long enough to fall in love with a girl much younger than himself – Isabel Riquelme. It was a brief idyll and in Chillan in August 1788 a son was born to the unmarried Isabel. He was born on the feast of St Bernard and was named Bernardo O'Higgins. Ambrosio was not too keen on the facts of his association with a Creole girl becoming known so he kept away from her and his son. But the result of any relationship fathered by the spirited

Ambrosio was not likely to stay in the background very long. Young Bernardo was sent off to London where he was likely to be kept in his place, but even that failed and when the young man's activities there became too embarrassing the Viceroy wrote a letter cutting him off from home, family – and worst of all – from money.

Bernardo never bore his father any malice and he wrote long letters from London. He became more aware than ever of his Irish blood and decided that his task in life would be, like that of most Irishmen, liberation. Liberation of his country from the Spanish domination. He set off for Chile and arrived home in the hope of some sort of reconciliation with his father. But Don Ambrosio was dead – and Irishman to the end he had died the day after St Patrick's Day, 1801. And, it was generally accepted, after a good party to celebrate Ireland's national day.

Bernardo went back to his hometown Chillan and became Mayor but all the time he was brooding on the injustices of the Spanish régime. He began to raise his own group of patriots and, in 1810, the revolution came. Now Bernardo O'Higgins found himself fighting the very men who had once supported his father. Frequently he found himself in tight corners but luck and a dogged resourcefulness was on his side. Plus a great deal of courage. Faced on one occasion by a group of over a thousand Royalist soldiers, O'Higgins could only muster two hundred men, but he stayed to fight. With a roar of 'Let the brave follow me!' he dashed into the oncoming forces and soon had then running in retreat.

He was a national hero long before his partnership with General San Martin of Peru won the final battle. In one battle he led not just an army but fifty thousand men, women and children, the whole population of a large province, on foot, donkeys, mules and horses against the Viceroy of Peru.

O'Higgins's private army won – and seven years after the first outbreak of civil violence he was elected President of Chile. Before he died he was not only honoured in his own country but in Peru as well, and today they still sing songs of O'Higgins and his deeds; streets, plazas, public buildings, hotels – even a whole province and a mountain – carry his name and honour one of the most romantic stories in Chilean literature, the story of the penniless boy who became the country's saviour.

It would be too much to expect that a man with the name of O'Higgins should fight a war without the help of other Irishmen – in his battle for freedom from Spain there were Irish on both sides. One of the leading rebel generals was Juan MacKenna – a man whose descendants still hold leading posts in the country. The men were recruited by special agents who were sent to Ireland to talk the Irish into fighting for yet another land's freedom. The recruiting sergeants were familiar figures in the land – they were there from Austria, Spain, France and South America.

One of the most successful of these recruiting agents was John Devereux (or D'Evereux) who had been exiled for his part in the 1798 rising. He was quick to realise the possibilities and when he met General Bolivar in Haiti he offered to raise an Irish Legion to fight on his side. His boast that he could recruit five thousand may have surprised Bolivar but it didn't cause any alarm to Devereux . . . who as well as raising the army raised a small fortune for himself. He also gained his share of fame and decided that a man was nothing without a title. His style took some beating and very soon plain John Devereux was 'Member of the Order of Liberators, Major General of the Army of the Republics of Venezuela and New Granada, commanding the Irish Legion'. His title carried the gulp of grandeur that the Latin temperament appreciated and soon they had added to it when the Colombian Government made him envoy to the Courts of Northern Europe. His luck seemed to be always running on a good high tide and he got himself out of many tough scrapes on his perambulations through Europe. But he had to thank the Irish-born Wellington for finally saving him from death in Italy where he was accused of taking part in the Latin-American uprising. Freed on Wellington's request he went back to America – but this time to North America where he lived on a pension from the Venezuelan Government until he died in 1854. His body was brought back to South America and laid in the National Pantheon at Caracas. There were few men who managed to please so many governments.

But if O'Higgins and Devereux seem to have collected all the glory in the South American campaigns there were others, too, who made their mark without the same rewards. San Martin's aide-de-camp, John Thomond O'Brien, from Cork, fought all through the campaign and after clearing the way for the General to march over the Andes still managed to be in on the battle of Chacabuco where he captured the Spanish Standard single-handed. O'Brien fought on with different armies in South America until he was an old man. Then there were others – like Daniel Francis O'Leary, a Colonel in the army of Bolivar, later Colombian envoy to the US, later still Venezuelan Minister to Spain, but remembered most of all for his memoirs of Bolivar. He was very close to the General – not only on his own word but on that of many visitors to the General's camp. One English officer who arrived with dispatches at Angosture found this scene:

> I went into the room which was large, but dirty, and scantily provided with furniture. At the further end sat Colonel O'Leary, then one of his Excellency's secretaries, on the ground with a small writing desk in his lap, writing

> dispatches of a military nature at the dictation of Bolivar, who, at the other end of the room, was sitting on the edge of a large South American cot, slung from the ceiling. To avoid the inconvenience of the heat, he was quite unencumbered with apparel or covering of any description . . .

And you can't get any closer to a general than that . . .

PART 3

A Woman's Place

CHAPTER I

Fickle . . . and Fighting

If the versatility of the soldiers, rebels, gold diggers and Indian fighters was ever in danger of being doubted, the women of Ireland would easily have saved the country's honour. They came up the hard way and when faced with the dangers to their husbands and families fought to the death – seldom displaying that expected trait of in-built feminine charity. They proved that at times they were fiercer than the males, less likely to look on fighting as a game and certainly less likely to stick to the accepted rules of the game. With the instinct to fight for her young the female of Ireland proved that Kipling knew his history when he wrote that 'the female of the species is more deadly than the male'.

There was a certain Elizabeth Fitzgerald who was besieged in her castle by a large if ill-armed tribe of Cahills. Mistress Fitzgerald showed every sign of being able to take care of herself and her castle, but the same could hardly be said of her husband. He wandered away from the castle and fell into the hands of the enemy. The Cahills thought they knew their woman and they brought the prisoner to the castle gates.

'We have your husband here,' they shouted, 'but we're willing to do a trade – we'll let you have him back if you will let us have the castle. And if you don't let us have the castle your husband will be throttled in front of your eyes in half an hour.'

Half an hour went past and then Elizabeth came out on to the castle wall. 'Mark the words of Elizabeth Fitzgerald,' she told the Cahills, 'for they may serve for your own wife on some future occasion. I won't render my castle and I'll tell you why – Elizabeth Fitzgerald may get another husband, but Elizabeth Fitzgerald may never get another castle. So I'll keep what I have.'

She kept to her word and so did the Cahills – in a short time the Squire was seen dangling by the neck from a nearby tree.

How Elizabeth Fitzgerald fared after that is not recorded, but she showed the singlemindedness that is evident in the Irish female from Queen Maeve, who boasted in the half-mystical past that she had fifteen hundred royal mercenaries, to Bernadette Devlin, in the half-mystical present, who called the people of Ulster to her barricades. Between these two there were women who terrorised land and sea, who followed men to the front and fought beside them, who put on uniforms and boasted of killing men – there is even a record of some fighting Irish nuns in the American civil war.

The earliest picture of just how the women of Ireland managed in times of war comes from a sixth century law tract. It establishes the place of women on the battlefront in a stark and dramatic way.

> The work which the gentlewoman had to do was to go to battle and battlefield encounter and to camping and to fighting and to hosting and to wounding. On one side she would carry her bag of provisions and on the other her babe. Her wooden pole upon her back; thirty foot long it was and had at one end an iron hook which she thrust into the tresses of some woman in the opposite battalion.

And if the woman showed any reluctance to fight she was herded in front by the men with a stick with 'which he hit her to make her fight'. And she had good reason to fight well for the rest of the law says that head and breasts were the trophies of war.

But hovering in the wings was a man named Adamnan whose ways were to eventually earn him a sainthood. The old tract goes on to depict how he came to grips with the women's problem. Once Adamnan and his mother were wending their way by Drogheda. 'Come upon my back, dear mother,' saith he.

'I shall not go,' saith she.

'What is this? What ails you,' saith he.

'Because you are not a dutiful son,' saith she.

'Who is more dutiful than I am? Since I put a girdle over my breast, carrying you about from place to place keeping you from urine and wet. I know of no duty which a son of man could do to his mother that I do not do for you; except the humming tune which women perform because I cannot perform that tune I will have a sweet-sounding harp made.'

'Even so,' saith she, 'your dutifulness were good, however that is not the duty I desire, but this that you should free women for me from the battle and the battlefield encounter, from the camping, from the hosting, from the wounding and from the bondage of the cauldron.'

Then she went upon her son's back and they chanced to come upon a battlefield. Such was the thickness of the slaughter into which they came that the soles of one woman touched the neck of another. Though they beheld the battlefield, they saw nothing more touching or more pitiful than the head of a woman in one place and the body in another, and her little babe upon the breast of the corpse, a stream of milk upon one of its cheeks and a stream of blood upon the other.

Later that night Adamnan had a dream in which an angel gave the law to him that became known as Adamnan's law or the Cain Adamnan, Ireland's earliest known law tract. 'Go forth into Ireland,' the angel said, 'and make a law in it that women shall not be killed in any way by men, through slaughter or by any other death either by poison or in the fire or in water or by any beast or by dogs, but that they shall die in lawful bed.'

But the lawful bed wasn't an absolute attraction – there were still women who showed more relish for the battle than the bed. They took their lead from Macha – a redheaded giantess of unusual accomplishment. The legend says that she wore 'a heavy cloak clasped upon her right shoulder with a great brooch in order that her strong right arm should remain free'. She was feminine enough not to follow the pattern set by the Amazons – she didn't have her breast cut off to give her more freedom of movement in battle. She was Queen of Ulster by conquest – and, fighter though she was, she still knew how to use her feminine charms.

On one occasion after routing an army led by her nephews she followed the five of them. So that they would not recognise her, she dressed as a leper. She caught up with them in some woods and so won them with her wit and knowledge that one of them followed her into the undergrowth to make love to her. But when they were out of earshot, she bound and gagged him. When she went back to the others they asked about the missing brother. She told them he was ashamed to return since he was captivated by the come-hither looks of a leper. 'He need not be ashamed,' they said 'since we all have been captivated by the beauteous lustre of your eyes.' One by one she invited them into the undergrowth – and when she got them there she tied them up. Then she marched them back to her palace.

Very much in the mould of the giantess was Anne Bonny, a girl who relished a battle as much as male company; only instead of the undergrowth she made her conquests on sea.

Anne was born in the seaside town of Kinsale, the daughter

of a lawyer but still outside the law. She travelled with her father halfway round the world and then met up with a poor specimen of a husband who took her round part of the other half and – unluckily for both of them – stopped off in the island of Providence on the West Indies. There Anne 'became acquainted with Rackham the pirate who making courtship to her, soon found means of withdrawing her affection from her husband so that she consented to elope with him and to go to sea in men's clothes'.

To sea they went and became the terror of every honest running ship in the ocean and it is recorded 'that when any business was to be done in their way, nobody was more forward or courageous than she'.

Inevitably they were captured and taken to be hanged but Anne was discovered to be pregnant at the time and she was reprieved. Not so lucky was Rackham; on the day of his execution he looked to his pirate queen for solace but she turned on him and in the style of Mrs Elizabeth Fitzgerald told him that if he had fought like a man he wouldn't have had to die like a dog. Poor consolation to Rackham.

Anne Bonny probably dreamed of being a second Grainne O'Malley, sea queen of Connemara, and one of the few women in history who thumbed their noses at Queen Elizabeth I. Grainne, in most history books, is little more than a tough woman pirate, but around the west coast of Ireland even today you can walk to the top of a hill and see the lookout posts she built or go out to the lonely islands in the Atlantic and see the remains of the castles she built. Grainne is one of the great female legends of Ireland, one that Hollywood has overlooked. A complete description of Grainne would be hard to define: she was a sort of feminine Rob Roy, a chieftainess, a princess of the sea.

She was about nineteen when her father died and, proud in

her boast that only the greatest O'Malleys ruled the Western Islands, she disinherited her brother and took her father's position for herself. She quickly proved her mettle; no ship was safe as soon as it trespassed on her domain and as most of those trading in and out of Galway had to enter O'Malley water Grainne filled her cupboards with treasures and wines of the best. It was even said that when she went to bed she kept a line tied from the boats to her toes to make sure that no one dared move one.

Not that she spent all her time at sea – she took off enough time to be married – twice. The first time was to an O'Flaherty whose reputation earned him the name of Ferocious. Even today there is a saying in the West of Ireland, 'From the ferocious O'Flahertys may the Good Lord deliver us.' Obviously his reputation didn't bother Grainne: she used her man to help her amass an even greater fortune. She also started her family with O'Flaherty and the story is told that the day the first baby was due news came in of a Turkish corsair sailing along the coast. Not one to miss a piece of action, Grainne decided to go with the vessel and soon the deck above her cabin was loud with the clashing of swords and the running of feet. Afraid for her own ship's safety she decided to join in, and with a pistol in each hand and a great blanket wrapped around her she strode on to the deck.

The sight of this extraordinary figure must have been enough to frighten even her own men – certainly it petrified the Turks – and Grainne, not one to miss even half a chance let go both barrels and shot down the Turkish officers. Seeing their officers shot and confronted by this astonishing figure, the Turkish sailors ran away panic-stricken, some even diving into the sea rather than face up to the gaunt-faced Grainne with her blazing guns.

When the ship was plundered Grainne went back to her cabin to give birth to her son. She christened him Theobald of the Long Ships.

Her first marriage didn't last long after this and soon she was looking around for another husband. She took the very rich Richard Bourke – Iron Dick to the natives – and part of their marriage agreement was that either one could say to the other at the end of a year 'I dismiss you' and the marriage was ended. Not for a minute expecting anything unusual, Sir Richard had agreed. A year later he had every reason to be sorry for his indiscretion. Grainne had manned all his strongholds with her own men and as he rode home one day when the year was up she gave him a curt dismissal; which sent him off to seek his fortunes in a more comfortable bed.

Now with castles on the islands, fortresses on the land and galleons on the sea Grainne was a powerful figure in the west, but ceaseless wars, jealousies and strife made her life a precarious one. She knew that at any time the British might decide she was just too powerful. So with a somewhat uncharacteristic gesture she offered part of her fleet to Elizabeth's Lord Deputy, Sir Henry Sydney, who wrote this description of her visit:

> There came to me also a most famous feminine sea-captain called Grany i Mallye and offered her service unto me wheresoever I would command her with three galleys and 200 fighting men in Ireland or Scotland . . . This was the most notorious woman in all the coast of Ireland.

Another description of Grainne was left by Sir William Drury: '. . . a woman who hath imprudently passed the parts of womanhood and had been a great despoiler and chief commander and director of thieves and murderers.' She was also described as 'a woman of the western province famous for her stoutness of courage and person, and for sundry exploits done by her at sea'.

Grainne seems to have believed that the submission she offered to Elizabeth's deputy was nothing more than an informal pleasantry, and she spent a great deal of her time fighting off British armies and ships.

One commander said scornfully, 'She thinketh herself no small lady' and discovered there was more to it than that when he sent a force into her domain to collect rents. When the commander met Grainne, she 'did swear to have my life for coming so far into their country'. But when faced with a full force of soldiers Grainne had to withdraw her threat, and she went with the commander to the British Governor and paid the rent.

Her troubles with the British had taken a turn for the worse and it wasn't long before her gallivanting on sea and land called down the wrath of the 'Black Jack' Bingham, Governor of Connaught. She was taken prisoner and, tied with a rope, was marched to Galway for sentence. But one of her in-laws went bail for her and back she went to terrorising Connemara.

Her offer to help the British was eventually accepted and soon the O'Malley ships were patrolling the western waters on behalf of two Queens – Grainne on her Clare Island fortress and Elizabeth in her Hampton Court palace. But no doubt the seamen knew to which queen they really owed allegiance.

Word of the extraordinary sea-queen soon filtered through to London and in 1592 there came an invitation for Grainne to go there. Away she sailed in her own fleet; around the Irish coast; across the Irish sea; around the toe of England and up the Thames in all majesty. They anchored below Tower Bridge and Grainne was taken to Queen Elizabeth, at Hampton Court. Why she was there has never been established. One report was that she went at Elizabeth's invitation – another that she went pleading for her son's release from a British jail. Whichever it was, Grainne, not one to be taken in by jewels, farthingales or magnificence, announced herself as 'Grainne O'Malley, chief of the country of Doodaro, O'Malley, called Owle O'Malley, now called the

Barony of Murasky'. She failed to mention her castles at Inishbofin, Inishshark, Inishturk or Clare Island but no doubt she gave the Queen of England to understand that she could have added these. She then thrust out her hand to Elizabeth and sat down without being asked.

Many stories have been added about that trip to London, probably a distance from the truth, but they still show the sort of woman who came from the wild west. Once an old storyteller in Cleggan, an O'Malley stronghold in Connemara, told me the story in his own way:

'The Queen of England then gave her a present.

' "What is it," says Grania.

' "It's a dog," said the Queen of England.

' "A dog, be the holy," said Grania, looking at the sad little patch of life that was being held to her.

' "A dog," said the other Queen. "It's a playful little thing and will live in your lap."

' "My lap," says Grania, "is never idle enough for a dog to be sitting in it. Keep it yourself, Queen of the English, 'tis only fit for idlers like yourself. You may fool the day away with such vermin."

'Well, the poor Queen of the English didn't know what to be doin' with herself, so she says to Grania.

' "I want to make you a countess."

' "Oh you can't do that," says Grania.

' "Why not," says Elizabeth.

' "Because I'm a Queen meself – the same as yourself."

'And do you know this, I'll hand it to the Queen of the English, she laughed and the two of them became great friends. Now if it had been the other way about what do you think would have happened?'

So the legends and stories of Grainne live on today in Connemara, stories that are softened with time but still retain some of the ruthlessness that O'Malley of the Isles passed on to his young daughter.

CHAPTER 2

Travelling Women

WHILE GRAINNE O'MALLEY stayed at home to marry her men and worry the law, other women found that, like Anne Bonny, there was a lot to be said for moving away with your man and seeing the world. But the travelling wasn't always easy; like the men they found that they too were expected to be able to look after themselves. They shared a common heritage of impulsiveness – and tenacity of character. They also had the itchy-foot tendency of the male of the race and were frequently found side by side with their husbands on the battlefront. Colonel W W H Davis of the 104th Pennsylvania Volunteers met one of them:

> An Irish camp woman, belonging to a New York Regiment, made herself quite conspicious during the action. She remained close to the side of her husband and refused to retire to a place of security. Occasionally she would notice some fellow sneaking up to the rear, when she would run after him, seize him by the nape of the neck, and place him in the ranks again, calling him 'a dirty, cowardly spalpeen', and other choice epithets. The flying shells had no terror for her. During the hottest of the cannonade this courageous woman walked fearlessly among the troops, encouraging them to stand up to their work. Her only weapon, offensive or defensive, was a large umbrella she carried under her arm.

Far more on the offensive was Kit Welsh, a woman who became one of the most extraordinary soldiers to fight in the British Army. She too had husband trouble. Kit's husband had been duped on board a British ship in Dublin in 1692. He was picked up in a typical Dublin recruitment drive for the British forces in those days. Military conditions were generally so bad that recruiting sergeants toured the pubs in the evening and cajoled drunks into signing on. 'He took the Saxon shilling' was the most denigrating comment anyone could make to or about an Irishman. As soon as they accepted the shilling – and spent it – they were packed on board a ship and cruised off to the nearest war. Often the 'recruits' were never heard of again – but some like Richard Welsh did write home after a few months. When eventually his wife got his letter, it was to say that he was very sorry for what had happened but he was in such a state that he could not really remember the circumstances. Anyway, he was a private in the British Army and as they had his signature there was little or no hope of his getting out until the wars were over.

What thousands of Dublin women in the same position did was to pine away and hope one day the good Lord – or the British – would send back their husbands in at least as good a condition as when they went away. But not Kit Welsh. Dick meant a great deal to her. She made her plans, bought a sword and a suit, and, masquerading as a man, began to travel in the wake of the British Army, wherever it fought, in the hope of meeting her husband again.

For ten years she searched, through the most devastating battles, and at the end all she had to show for it were four sword, shot and bayonet wounds. She was captured too, but escaped. And all the time no one guessed that this fierce fighting soldier was the missus from Dublin looking for a wandering husband. She fought in Marlborough's army and it is recorded that when the great general was told eventually that this brave soldier was really a woman he had the shock of his life. When someone added that she left two children behind in Dublin, Marlborough must have been shattered.

Kit's wanderings eventually brought her reward: at the battle of Landen she saw Dick again. It was a fierce moment in the battle and he was in a trench across the way from her. With a ferocity that many a man would have envied, she got up and ran to him, but within yards of his trench she was shot down. Dick Welsh didn't realise that the soldier who had been shot down almost beside him was his wife, to him it was just another casualty of the war – he fought on for his own life.

The army moved on with Kit among the injured, and they were parted again. Her next adventure took her to a Dutch town where she defended a young girl from a guardsman with rape on his mind. Defending the girl meant a duel, which Kit won. She sent the sergeant away injured and for this was thrown into prison, but the young girl, who had taken quite a fancy to the soldier who had fought for her honour, intervened, and when she told the full story Kit was released, still without anyone knowing she was a woman. She had really to run then, to avoid what could have been an embarrassing affair.

Back to war she went – still as a man. And again, despite injuries in battles, she managed to keep her sex a secret. Then one day in an inn, she thought she recognised the man playing about with a damsel on his knee. It was Dick, and never a more surprised man had a girl whisked out of his arms to be faced by his 'forgotten' wife. But Kit was so delighted at finding Dick that she forgave him and there the story should have ended. But Kit found now that she loved the life with the army better than that of the conventional wife. She decided to stay on. So, as comrades, they fought side by side. A year passed – then came the battle that gave the secret way. Kit was wounded again, and the doctors found out her sex. But everyone was so taken with the whole story of her fighting, which was now almost a byword in the army, that they decided not only to forgive her but to see that Dick and herself had a second wedding—with full regimental honours.

After the second wedding Kit became camp cook, but she never was far away from Dick. She was there one day with his food when three French soldiers tried to jump her man. She whipped up a fallen musket and blew the three of them to eternity. The only injury she had to show for the encounter was a broken front tooth – hit by a shot.

Dick was killed soon after this but Kit was not a girl to miss an opportunity and soon she was married to her husband's best friend. But this marriage didn't last long for he too was killed a few months later.

When she was forty-three, Kit was drafted home. Her reputation had gone before her, Queen Anne and Marlborough received her and she was granted a pension of a shilling a day. With this money, it wasn't surprising that she was soon married again – but for the third time Kit was unlucky. Her latest husband had a liking for the drink. He signed on in the army for a shilling during one of his bouts and Kit had to set out to earn enough money, selling pies and beer in Westminster, to buy his discharge. There was a great celebration the day his freedom came, but he spoiled it all by getting drunk and signing on again! He quietened down after that and lived to be admitted to Chelsea Hospital as a pensioner in 1717. Kit was admitted too, and when she died in 1739 she was buried at St Margaret's, Westminster, with full military honours.

Kit's courage and persistence had taken her across ten of

Europe's fiercest battlefields in twenty years but, despite the fighting and the soldier's uniform, her instincts were always feminine. Her man was out there too. It was a precedent that had been set by so many Irishwomen before, and one that was to be repeated often in the next two hundred years. For some, there was more than a mere place in the Chelsea Pensioners' Home at the end of their fighting; sometimes there was a crown, a throne or a title. Sometimes they knew this was their reason for fighting; others got different rewards as a just return for their endeavours. But few of the fighting Irishwomen equalled the fantastic story of Eliza Lynch, the wonder and toast first of Paris and then, for a different reason, of South America. She took her 'wifely duties so much to heart that she followed her husband to war with her own brigade of Amazons.

The famine of 1845 drove the Lynch family out of Ireland and, like so many before them, they landed in France hoping to retrieve their lost fortunes in the Second Empire. But they only managed to scrape a mere existence and when, at fourteen, young Eliza decided that she wanted to marry a veterinary surgeon of good prospects, the family raised no objections. But the church and the law of France raised objections, so Eliza moved to England and at Folkestone on 3rd June 1850 she was married to Monsieur Quatrefages.

Her determination that nothing would ever cause her to live the life her family had fled from in Ireland, bred in her during the next couple of years a hardness and a desire for nothing but the best. Her husband, however, turned out to be a more settled type and when he found that business was good enough for him in North Africa, Eliza wasn't wholly in agreement. She became bored, packed a few bags and took herself back to France. There her stunning beauty soon became the talk of the town and she discovered a new and easy way to live life as she had always dreamed. She set herself up in an opulent apartment; the silks and braids and satins of the time tumbling around her; she added a marble bathroom with silver fittings. Nothing was too good for Eliza Lynch when there were men fighting each other to pay for her rent and keep. Her private room opened up a wider stream of riches – she installed herself in a plush *salon* with gaming tables and soon the patronage became even wider and richer. And in the new patrons there was one – a South American – who was richer, more handsome and more to Eliza's fancy than any of the others. His name was Francisco Solano López, son of the President of Paraguay, and the thousands of pounds that had changed hands in Miss Lynch's *salon* were forgotten as she set her sights on him.

He became infatuated with Eliza and took her first on a grand tour of Europe and then home to South America. If Eliza Lynch had been an interesting woman in Paris, here she was a sensation. This tall, blonde, beautiful woman was completely new – no one had ever seen anyone so fair before. But not everyone was impressed. Least of all the President. He hardly acknowledged Eliza.

Francisco's mother could only wail: 'Why could you not have taken a girl from our own country?' To which he replied: 'She is a great lady. I will marry her when her husband lets her go free.'

This only shocked the South American President and family even more. He decided that they must get rid of the Irishwoman. He plotted and schemed but somehow Eliza was taking a grip in the city of Asunción. She began to change the architecture of the city, had an opera house built, a library, a post office and, doubtless with plans well laid, a whole new palace. Her relations with Francisco never changed and she gave birth to a son; her next child, a daughter, died while still a baby.

When the President died Francisco took office. He immediately set Eliza up as he would a legal wife and insisted that she be accorded all privileges that normally went to a women in her position. For ten years Eliza and Francisco lived in Paraguay in relative happiness and peace and their family increased. Then war came. The President led troops into Brazil, and while he was away he appointed Eliza Regent of Paraguay. At first the war went well but soon Francisco suffered reverses. Immediately Eliza formed her own army of women, dressing them in military jackets and skirts and trimming their heads with multi-coloured ribbons. When word came through that her husband was ill Eliza marched at the head of her army to his assistance.

Even when he recovered Francisco found that Madame Lynch was not too keen to leave him and she fought with her Amazons by his side. They were in camp together with a small force one day when a Brazilian platoon swooped down. López fled but Eliza stayed behind. Seeing a group of her female warriors standing by she shouted at them to pick up arms, and mount their battle-weary and hungry horses. Then she shouted them into an attack on the Brazilians.

The sight of a troop of wild screaming women mounted on starving horses and flinging lances about their heads shattered the attackers – they fled. So Eliza and Francisco battled on . . . but in February 1870 López was killed as he was wading across a stream on horseback. Eliza was ahead in a coach with one of her sons when a soldier from Brazil caught up with them and told them Lopez was dead. Her son made to avenge his father but the soldier was quicker and with a lance thrust killed the boy who fell across his mother's knees.

Eliza was escorted back to the spot where López lay dead and there she was made to dig a rough grave for her husband and son. She was only thirty-six years old.

Exiled then to Europe by the Brazilians she spent years alone in Paris and on 25th July 1886 she died – penniless. The Municipality of Paris paid for her burial at Père Lachaise.

But she was not completely forgotten in South America – there were still people who talked of the golden-haired Irish woman who fought through many a rugged battle with them. But it was fifty years until justice was done to her. Her remains were carried reverently back to Asunción and with a lowering of flags and a last post she was laid in the Pantheon de los Héroes in the city where she had virtually been queen.

CHAPTER 3

Madame, the Countess

IF IT IS a flamboyant heroine you want – one who is dramatic, swashbuckling, swaggering and notorious all at once – there is really only one women who can fill the bill. Her name Countess Markievicz, once Constance Gore-Booth, once 'The Red Countess' but always in Irish mouths either 'Madame' or 'The Countess'. The piracy of Anne Bonny, the rebellious Grainne O'Malley, fade when confronted with this extraordinary woman. She strode across a brilliant period of Irish history from the late nineteenth century right into the first quarter of the twentieth with verve, passion and character which will multiply with the years giving her a place foremost in any story of Ireland's fighters. She will emerge from any analysis as one of the most complicated characters of the Irish race – she will be seen as beautiful, menacing, lovable, dictatorial, courageous, ferocious, always militant, often kind, sometimes a killer.

Probably Yeats had the right word for Constance when he called the family 'inflammable' after a visit to their beautiful home at Lissadell in County Sligo in mid-1890. Sean O'Faolain saw her as '. . . one of the most gallant creatures our country had the good fortune to attract to her side at a time when only a very few supremely brave and generous-hearted men were, like her, glad to gamble their lives on the faith that Ireland's spirit was not dead but merely sleeping'. That was another factor in the story of the Countess: she was a gambler – not with other people's lives but with her own.

Born on 4th February 1868 – the firstborn of three famous sisters – her fearless horsemanship became one of the legends of Sligo by the time she was ten years old. She wrote a description of how she grew up: 'We lived on a beautiful, enchanted West Coast, where we grew up intimate with the soft mists and the coloured mountains and where each morning you woke to the sound of the wild birds . . .' There was no interest in politics in her home, yet in that soft environment Constance, the great political figure, grew up. In 1898 she went to Paris to study art and almost to starve, in the accepted way, in a garret. She met there a Polish Count, Casimir Markievicz. They married, even though he had less to see them through life, materially, than Constance.

She gave birth to a daughter back in Dublin, but soon the child was passed on to governesses and nursemaids – the political feelings of the country were taking control of her. She was forty; a famous, if unpronounceable, name to Dubliners. The women who gathered to give their time to helping with the revolution were understandably suspicious of this extraordinary woman who came among them. She must have seemed so out of place with her Anglo-Irish accent, her Big House ways, and her authoritarian ambitions. But, at last, the Daughters of Erin accepted her.

Slowly the great pulse of the Rising built up and when the explosion came, Countess Markievicz strode out in the dark-green uniform jacket that had been cast off by Commandant Michael Mallin as too small for even his slight figure. But it fitted the Countess. On her head she wore a slouch hat with a great plume of cock's feathers – her own design and one that must have made her one of the most distinguishable targets in the whole Revolt. Her husband, the Count, had earlier gone to

Countess Markievicz – dramatic, swashbuckling, passionate, dictatorial – probably the most fascinating woman in the history of Ireland.

Facing page 144]

Sir John Moore – his death on the battle field has been honoured in song and story – even the French, defeated at Corunna where Moore lost his life, recognising the Irishman's fighting merits, raised a monument over his remains.

– From an engraving by C. Turner.

Marshal MacMahon – an astute soldier with a long and varied experience of war – served the French well.

In an ordinary Army tent at the headquarters of the British 21st Army Group, on May 4th, 1945, Field Marshal Montgomery reads out the surrender terms to the German leaders. Seated at the table are (left to right) Rear-Admiral Wagner, General Admiral Von Friedeburg, Commander-in-Chief of the Germany Navy and leader of the surrender delegation; and Field-Marshal Montgomery. With backs to camera are Colonel Poleck (left) and General Kinzel.

fight in the name of Poland at the outbreak of the First World War; her child was being cared for; her family worried for her, and well they might for this was the hour she had been awaiting. 'Our heart's desires were granted to us,' she said, 'and we counted ourselves lucky.'

She wasn't the only woman in the Rising on that Easter Monday, 1916, when Dublin was taken over in the most daredevil of all the Irish revolts. There were many others but only two held commissions – the Countess and Dr Kathleen Lynn, who had the medical rank of captain. In the Countess's company was Margaret Skinnider, who came over from Scotland in December 1915 and brought with her some detonators for 'the cause'. They weren't sure how to use the detonators so, wrote Margaret, 'Madame and I went up to the Dublin mountains to try them out and succeeded in blowing up an old wall.' But now there was more than an old wall to blow up – the whole eight-hundred-year reign of the British was under fire.

At first the Countess was only expected to tour the city in a car with Dr Lynn and look after the casualties, but when she was driving through St Stephen's Green, her friend, Commandant Mallin, called her. He said he was so desperately short of men that he needed her as a sniper. She was delighted at the opportunity and there and then Mallin promoted her to second-in-command. The small band then marched to the College of Surgeons where they rang the bell to gain admittance. But no one answered. The Countess took out her revolver and blew the lock away. The Citizen's army had taken control.

When the British troops got over the shock of the Rising they set out to stamp it down. In St Stephen's Green they mounted machine guns on the Shelbourne Hotel making all outdoor positions in the area untenable; the Irish retired to the College of Surgeons with the Countess and Mallin. It became something of a fortress and the main fighting that came from it was in the form of sniping with the odd foray out into the streets in search of food, supplies and news of how the Rising was going in other parts of the city. Margaret Skinnider remembers once seeing the Countess and a man named Partridge move out of the building; approaching along a nearby street was a troop of British soldiers.

> The Countess stood motionless waiting for them to come near . . . and in her officer's uniform and black hat and great plumes, looked most impressive. At length she raised her gun to her shoulder – it was an automatic which she had converted into a short rifle – and took aim. Neither she nor Patridge noticed me. I was quite close when they fired. The shots rang out at the same moment, and I saw the two officers leading the column drop to the street.

This was the first time that there is any record of the Countess killing anyone in the fighting. She was to go out again later when Margaret Skinnider was wounded – this time to avenge her friend's injury. 'Soon after I was brought in,' wrote Margaret Skinnider, 'the Countess and Mr Partridge disappeared. They went into the street. There were only two soldiers there and they both fired. That gave Madame a chance to sight them. She fired twice and killed both.'

When the Leaders of the Rising surrendered and the message was passed to the Countess she wanted to disobey the order and fight on. 'Let us die at our posts,' she pleaded but Mallin replied that they had to obey orders. When the British came they offered her a seat in a car to take to jail but she refused and marched, beside Mallin, at the head of the group being taken away.

The leaders were courtmartialed and shot, Mallin among them. The Countess was sentenced to die too. In prison when the sentence was being read to her the Governor mumbled and stuttered, afraid to look her in the eyes. Turning on him she said: 'What's that you're saying, man! Read it again! I don't know what you're mumbling about.'

She was reprieved – because she was a woman – and her bitterness dissolved into tears when she heard that all the other leaders, including James Connolly, had been shot. 'Why didn't they let me die with my friends?' she asked. Instead they kept her in Mountjoy prison – then she was moved to Aylesbury. In Dublin even prison had its compensations, there were other Irish around her, but in England she found only cold, damp cells, uneatable food, one hour's exercise a day, incessant floor scrubbing; no friends, no one to discuss ideas with – she was sentenced to this for life.

She became the first woman to be elected to the British Parliament but she was still in prison and could not take her seat. She felt that there was little hope of her sentence being shortened. 'Don't count on my getting out of here for ever so long,' she wrote, 'unless a fuss is made (home and America). I don't see why they should let me go.' But release was inevitable and in 1917 all internees were released. Constance arrived home in Dublin to a tumultuous welcome; she stood in the back of Dr Lynn's car as it drove through the cheering crowds.

Her eventual reward was the post of Minister of Labour in de Valera's first cabinet. She said it wasn't a case of them giving the job to a woman. 'I took a gun to their heads,' she said – and no one was ever quite sure if she was in earnest or not. They remembered that she was very handy with revolver and rifle. But Ireland still wasn't free and it wasn't long before she was back in prison – this time for making 'seditious speeches'. For four months she was in Cork Jail and, being almost a connoisseur of prisons, reported that this one was 'the most comfortable one

I've been in yet'. When she came out she found that the Dail (the Government) was on the run but the Cabinet met secretly, despite British pressure, as often as possible. She wasn't long free before she found herself back in prison – this time sentenced to two years' hard labour, after being held for two months without trial. The charge was conspiracy and organising the killing of soldiers. She described the scene: 'One lone woman surrounded by bayonets and tin hats, facing innumerable accusing and judging men, last comic stroke, the Englishman in wig and gown, it must have looked awfully funny.' The truce of 1921 brought her release from Mountjoy once again – but there followed in Ireland the Civil War. And while editing the Republican paper, *Eire*, from Glasgow she was arrested, to spend another short term behind bars.

She died – she believed of appendicitis, others believe cancer – on 15th July 1927. Her friends and family were around her bedside. She found the gathering of so many loved ones 'beautiful – beautiful to have all this love and kindness before I go!'

She was given a great funeral, buried in the Republican plot in Glasnevin and Mr de Valera spoke the oration.

There are people today who would not only regard the Countess with horror but would be glad to see her forgotten. Give us instead the beauty of Maud Gonne McBride, Hanna Sheehy Skeffington, Mary MacSweeny they call, and there is no doubt that these women played a great part in the fighting and the formative years, but the Countess justified her position and her attitudes spectacularly. Her sister wrote about her:

When on the old world's scrap-heap flung
Powers and Empires pass away,
Radiant and unconquerable
Thou shalt be young.

But not everyone looks at the Countess with that touch of sentimentality – recently Ernest Blythe, a prominent supporter of the Rising said about her: 'She spoke hysterically at times and did take extreme lines. I had disliked her because I believed the yarn that she had shot British soldiers in 1916; well, I have no use for killer women.' Mr Blythe's dislike of the Countess was always apparent – he called her a show-off and said 'she spoke so hysterically and breathlessly that you'd expect nothing but folly from her'.

R M Fox, who died in 1970, would never agree with this rating of 'Madame'. When she spoke outside the country, Fox found she made a magnificent appeal, rising even to great heights. At home, he felt, she spoke to people more as a family to whom it was unnecessary to make any special appeal. He remembered her as a kind woman always ready to fight for the downtrodden; saving a young man from execution by pleading that he be allowed to go to America; lashing at a Lord who evicted a family because he wanted their home for an Orange Hall – she called him a cad masquerading as a nobleman; feeding the poor of Dublin during her own troubles. She could, he recalled, be the grand lady of perfection or the gamin of the guardroom – whichever role was called for. To the British she was an awkward woman, a dangerous one, the 'Red Countess' of sedition, conspiracy and even death. They were glad to be rid of her in the final handover of Ireland to the Irish. It is the way she would have liked to be remembered – the woman who helped to free Ireland.

PART 4

A Way to Fight

CHAPTER I

With a Shillelagh

THERE'S A SHRIVELLED piece of legend tucked away in every one of those small, black enamelled pieces of oak that tourists take home from Ireland nowadays. They masquerade under the name of shillelaghs, and are an indecent insult to the smooth, seasoned, lead-topped fighting stick peculiar to the country.

Three foot long, oak or blackthorn, seasoned in the chimney for six months, balanced with lead, massaged with goose fat, fastened to the wrist with a leather strap, the shillelagh was as much a part of the fighting Irishman as the sword was of the more sophisticated duellists. It wasn't the sort of weapon with which a man would swagger through a fair just to show off: it was no more brought out on peaceful occasions than a sword was unsheathed.

But when the blood was up the shillelagh would knock more sense into a man's head than any other contemporary weapon. And it was swung more with passion than in anger at fights which were known in every corner of Ireland at one time.

The faction fights were sometimes spontaneous, sometimes planned outbursts between families, tribes, districts or towns, but generally they seem to have taken place without any real discoverable cause. A cause which according to one writer sprung from a species of ambition that prevails in the Green Isle, an ambition to be boss in his own parish. The big fights were usually held after half-yearly fairs or festivals, and when they really got under way they provided battles that have made the name 'Donnybrook' a household word for something more than a tantrum, something less than a war.

Donnybrook was one of the old fairs where a faction fight was likely to prolong the occasion for days and keep the hucksters, tinkers, fiddlers, bards and all the panorama of the eighteenth century in joyous exultation. One bard put the words down and caught the atmosphere of the faction fights fairly well:

In ruxion delighting
Laughing – while fighting.

The Dublin Penny Journal of 1832, commented:

> An Irishman cannot walk or wander, sport or fight, buy or sell, comfortably without an oak stick in his hand. If he travels he will beg, borrow or steal a shillelagh; if he goes to play he hurls with a crooked oak stick; if he goes to a fair it is delightful to hear the sound of his cloghel-peen on the cattle-norns; if he fights, as fight he must, the cudgel is brandished on high.

You weren't a man until you had your own shillelagh, and every boy equated a knowledge of faction fighting with that of his ABC – and in many cases considered it more important.

William Carlton wrote that there was scarcely a boy 'who had not before his fifteenth years, a just claim to be called the hero of a hundred fights, and the heritor of as many bumps on the cranium as would strike both Gall and Spurzheim speechless'.

Just about every writer of eighteenth- and nineteenth-century Ireland left behind details of faction fights which they witnessed. Some found that the fights were started by one group trailing a coat along the ground in front of their enemies; and as soon as the coat tail was stepped on the fight started. Another good beginning was when one man, called the bullyman because of his bullying ways, 'wheeled' or marched for his party up and down antagonising the others by whirling his shillelagh in the air and shouting, 'Here is Kelly, aboo, aboo – who'll dare to hit a Kelly.'

'I will,' would come the inevitable shout, 'a Murphy will hit the Kelly – Murphy aboo, aboo.'

Within minutes the whole area, marketplace, field or street would be in an uproar. The 'slashers' (the fighters) were in there swinging and roaring in the glory of the fight. The 'slashers' wore no real protection against the shillelagh other than a double-crowned cap of rabbit fur, something like a rugby scrumcap. Each side had its own band of 'seconds' or 'tallymen' who pulled the injured away from the fight and then with practised fingers probed the skull for any sign of 'softening of the head'. And in the bottle they carried there was always something stronger than water, something that would cure even the most battered skull.

Inglis in his *Irish Tour* presented a picture of one battle he witnessed in Galway between the Joyces and the Connemara boys. He was sitting in a tent drinking poteen – illicit whiskey with a kick like a torchlight procession – when

> some boastful expression of a Joyce appeared to give offence to several at the far end of the tent; and something loud and contentious was spoken of by two or three in a breath. The language, which, in compliment to me had been in English, turned to Irish. Two or three glasses of poteen were quickly gulped by most of the boys, and the innkeeper, who had accompanied me and sat by me, whispered that there would be some fighting. I had seen an abundance of fighting on a small scale in Ireland, but, I confess I had been

> barbarous to wish I might see a regular faction fight; and now I was likely to be gratified. Taking the hint of the innkeeper, I shook hands with the 'boys' nearest to me right and left; and taking advantage of a sudden burst of voices, I stepped over my bench and retiring from my tent took up a safe position on some neighbouring rocks.

And with the audience of one now safely hidden behind a rock, the Joyces and the Connemara 'boys' got down to it in earnest

> and the flourishing of shillelaghs did not long precede the using of them. Any one, to see an Irish fight for the first time, would conclude that a score or two must inevitably be put *hors de combat*. The very flourish of a regular shillelagh and the shout that accompanies it seem to be the immediate precursors of a fractured skull; but the affair, though bad enough, is not as fatal as it appears to be; the shillelaghs, no doubt, do sometimes descend upon a head, which is forthwith a broken head . . . but they oftener descend upon each other; and the fight soon becomes one of personal strength.

Which is as nice a piece of understatement as has been made about the faction fights – especially when Mr Inglis added, 'Nor is there any cessation of blows even when a man is on the ground.'

Not all faction fights finished with only a little 'head softening' – there were men killed and frequently there were cases of serious wounding. Various efforts were made to stop the fights but in most cases the local police, obviously knowing the cases at better hand than the resident Under-Secretary for Ireland, sat back and took a long draught from a mug of beer and didn't hear a word or a sound from the battle-racked streets outside their windows. One police report suggested that it was better if they stayed out of the way for if they stepped in it 'might end in bloodshed'!

Another suggestion came in a book, *Irish Disturbances*, by George Cornewall Lewis. He suggested that the local authorities encouraged faction fighting as 'it seemed to them that the people must necessarily raise their hands against someone; and they thought that factions would serve the same purpose as the stone thrown by Cadmus among the earthborn warriors of Thebes – that of turning the violence of the combatants themselves upon one another'.

Sometimes there were other peacemakers. W R le Fanu witnessed one fight: 'In vain the parish priest and his curate ride through the crowd, striking right and left with their whips; in vain a few policemen try to quell the riot; on it goes till one or other of the factions is beaten and flies.' Not always was it the opposition that was running away – le Fanu saw a young man running along the river bank after the fight, pursued by a much older man. Every time the old man got within striking range he swung his blackthorn on the already bloodied head of the youth.

'Why,' said le Fanu to another watcher, 'does that young fellow let the old man beat him in such a savage way?'

'Ah, sure, your honour,' came the reply, 'that's only his father is chastising him for fighting.'

There was an unwritten law in the fighting that opposite factions, who happened to dwell near each other, lived peacefully together, 'except on the occasions when they met expressly for a fight'. Now and again the law was broken and two factions carried on the fight in groups and on a personal basis for a long time.

In the West of Ireland there was, and I suppose there still is, a village named Moneen which once achieved the reputation of being 'what the Bowery and Chinatown are to New York'. This small village of thatched houses was the capital of the Gromastoons, 'a relentless people who would follow up a quarrel even to the very death', according to James Berry whose sketches of life in the West appeared in *The Mayo News* at the beginning of this century. (These sketches were later collected in book form and published by The Dolmen Press.) When the Gromastoons went to fight they could gather at least six hundred men and be sure of bringing three hundred women followers.

The big battle in Gromastoon lore was the fight between themselves and the Galvanaghs, but here there was at least a reason for the hatred. One day a Galvanagh schoolmaster thrashed a Gromastoon lad whose father was known as the 'Rebel' O'Donnell. The next day the Rebel turned up at the school, sorted out two Galvanagh 'professors' and 'thrashed the two venerable gentlemen within an inch of their lives'. After that, with his temper well and truly turkey red, O'Donnell roared: 'And I'll do the same to any other Galvanaghs in the parish.' It was the sort of threat that no schoolboy could possibly let go without telling his father, and very soon there was many a Galvanagh waiting for the right moment to make the Gromastoon man put actions to his words.

Unluckily for O'Donnell, he walked into it one day when he passed through the town of Bunowen, in the heart of the Galvanagh country. He was accosted by one of the Galvanagh men: 'Are you the man that whipped the two professors?' 'I am that,' said O'Donnell, 'and there's others I'd do it to as well.' And without trailing a coat or calling on a bullyman, the Galvanagh man set on O'Donnell and sent him home with the equivalent of a head softening.

No one in either parish would have been fool enough to

expect that the feud would end there. The two clans took sides and, according to Berry, 'they fought on Sundays and holidays, at fairs and patterns, at wakes and funerals, and for years every man carried his life in his hands, and even the military could not put the fighting down'.

For years the countryside around Louisburg in Mayo was in a state of siege . . . then on Christmas Day, 1829, came the faction fight to end all faction fights. At noon, word came through the village that the Gromastoons were marching nine hundred strong on the town of the Galvanaghs. There was almost despair in the town because many of the Galvanagh men had been to Midnight Mass and were scattered throughout the parish in their own homes. But horses were readied and riders went around the countryside recruiting all the Galvanaghs. In the town, the few fighting men that were available took up positions at the end of the main street, at the top of a small hill at a spot where they were sheltered by the gable ends of houses. Like a general, Billy Nicholson, the old man who led the Galvanaghs, placed his men strategically to meet the advancing clan.

Soon the peace of that Christmas Day was shattered as twelve hundred men fought each other with blackthorns and ash. The roar of the men in battle and the shrieks of women and children re-echoed through the town. But the Galvanagh men were coming in from the outlying parish in hordes to help their comrades and 'the Gromastoons began to fall in hundreds' and when they fell their womenfolk drew them down into a vacant space where the wounded were 'piled high'. When evening came the battle eased off and soon the Celtic wail for the dead could be heard. Stretched out in the street was a Gromastoon man, Jimmy Hoban, and the women gathered around him 'weeping . . . with the weird cries of so many banshees'.

This death seemingly ended the battle and the aggressors

retired, carrying their wounded with them, 'most of them maimed and disfigured for life, but the Galvanaghs scarcely had a scratch'. An inquest was held after the fight and, according to Berry, it resulted in the transportation of many for twenty years to Van Diemen's Land.

Where the Gromastoons of that battle had their wounds treated is not recorded, but le Fanu recorded that his family had a coachman who was considered the best of the amateur surgeons in their part of the south. This coachman had gleaned his medical knowledge when he had been a batman in the Peninsular War. 'His method was simple, somewhat painful and supposed by the sufferers to be highly efficacious. He clipped the hair from around the wound, poured in turpentine mixed with whiskey – this, of course, caused a yell – stitched the cut if a severe one, plastered it slightly, and then sent his patient home, equally amazed at his skill and charmed with his kindness.'

The amateur surgeon wasn't only called on after a faction fight – there were other fights, much in the same style but with a different intention. They were the funeral fights which generally occurred when two funerals were held on the same day in the same churchyard. There was an old superstition that the last person buried in a graveyard had, when he got to Purgatory (presuming he hadn't been cast for higher or hotter places) to carry water to allay the thirst of all those previously gone there. He kept his job until another soul arrived into the same graveyard. So if two funerals were bent for the same churchyard there was a great race to see which side would get there first. All sorts of ploys were used to hold up the other funeral and often it came to blows. Le Fanu remembers two funerals approaching a graveyard from opposite directions; one group began to run with their coffin across a field to reach the grave first and they just managed to get their coffin over the wall before the others.

Bernadette Devlin, MP for Mid-Ulster, smashes a rock behind the Londonderry barricades.

Facing page 160]

The Rev. Ian Paisley (hand aloft – centre) on the march.

British troops face more trouble in Ulster – 1972.

This was considered sharp practice and soon the fists were flying.

The superstitions took a lot longer to be killed than the faction fights but eventually the priests managed to stamp them out. Daniel O'Connell is said to be responsible for killing off the faction fights by appealing to Irishmen to stick together, and promising that the day wasn't far off when they could all join in the biggest faction of all – against the English. With the promise of such a shindig local rivalries were forgotten, but one priest recounted that the last dying words of many a countryman was a complaint that he wouldn't be living to trail his coat when 'the real affair' got under way.

O'Connell's promise was, unfortunately for many and lucky for some, a tame way for the tradition of the shillelagh fights to end.

CHAPTER 2

'I Can Lick Any Son of a Bitch'

Out from a land where the faction fights and the fist fights were frequent, stepped Peter Corcoran, bitter and pugnacious. If you can believe the contemporary prints he carried a look of perpetual surprise on his boyish features. And well he might, for while men dig a lifetime for gold and precious metals Corcoran stepped into the land of the Briton with nothing more to offer than the full of his fist. No doubt he was astounded to find out that here was a country where, instead of deporting you or throwing you into a prison to rot, they actually paid you to fight.

Corcoran landed in England just when prize fighting was coming into its own. The year was 1771 and in his first fight, with only one punch, Corcoran knocked out the reigning champion in one of the shortest ever bouts in the ring. As the giant Bill Darts lay flat on the floor of the wooden ring, the crowd, on their way to the Derby, saw the first professional Irish pugilist put his name on a title. For five years he held the heavyweight crown before he lost it in a questionable match in 1776.

But looking after himself without the benefit of little more than his raw fists was a way of life, part of the education of the men of the time in Ireland, and when word got back of Corcoran's success there was a flood of potential pugilists across the sea. Fight – and be paid for it, this was heaven. And the fighting was all in fun, or so it must have seemed anyway. It was four years before another Irishman got revenge on the man who beat Corcoran, but revenge it was and this time a boatswain by the name of Duggan Fearns won the heavyweight title in one and a half minutes – again with a first punch after which the then reigning champion 'declined to continue'.

The pattern was then set: the Irish were discovering their own capacity in the bare-knuckle fights. And what fights these were! In 1830, Simon Byrne handed out such a beating in forty-seven rounds that his opponent Sandy McKay died soon afterwards. Byrne was tried for manslaughter and acquitted. But only three years later he himself died after his fight for the British championship, with James (the Deaf 'un) Burke. The fight lasted for ninety-nine rounds in a soul-destroying three hours and sixteen minutes, the longest championship fight on record.

It was at this point that the fighting world of Britain and America came together. Burke was hounded out of England after Byrne's death and found himself in the States. There he came up against the American set – which was even there dominated by the Irish, both honest and crooked. The leader was Samuel O'Rourke, a gambler and gangster, who swore to do Burke injury. There was a running battle when a fight was arranged between the two of them and it only ended after the hot-tempered crowd drew guns on one another. Burke escaped only to lose his next fight to another Irishman, Paddy O'Connell.

Thus the Irish dominance of the American ring was confirmed, although O'Rourke didn't last long in command. He lost heavily at gambling, couldn't pay and was eventually found in a dark corner . . . murdered. This didn't put the Irish off. In boat loads they were hurrying away from the more positive death of the

Famine. The ring provided money and opportunity and one of the first to cash in was James Ambrose, who took the name Yankee Sullivan for fighting. Behind him came, what Nat Fleischer, editor of *The Ring*, called the wave of Irish supremacy. John Morrison, from Tipperary, fought with his fists and eventually landed in Tammany Hall and became the first fighter to be elected to Congress. John Carmel Heenan came next, then Mike McCool, Joe Coburn, Ned O'Baldwin, Johnny Dwyer and Paddy Ryan . . . all opening the way for the challenging roar of John L Sullivan: 'I can lick any son of a bitch in the world.'

Sullivan, reckoned by Nat Fleischer to be the champion of champions, was in his day the supreme fist fighter and labelled 'the greatest fighter in eternity'. He met and beat every fighter worthy – and unworthy – of the name, in a fantastic ten year sprawl of boastfulness, determination, strength, showmanship and guile. The writers who insisted there 'will never be another John L Sullivan' had their crystal balls well adjusted – there never was another fighter quite like him.

John Laurence Sullivan was the son of Michael Sullivan from Tralee, County Kerry, and his wife who came from the town of Athlone on the Shannon. How Mr and Mrs Sullivan ever came to be matched is one of the mysteries of love: he was 5ft 3½ inches and topped the scale at 130 pounds; his wife, according to John L's own description was a woman of 'a fair size . . . weighing 180 pounds . . . she was considered a woman of remarkable physical and mental powers'. John L was born on 15th October 1858. He was brought up in the tough school of the Boston Irish and recorded that his first real fight was with a school pal when they were both fourteen; he only gave up that particular scrap when he was frightened of the flow of blood from his opponent's nose – something that was never to stand in his way again. Eventually it became an honour to have been knocked out by Sullivan, and the old picture is often presented of an Irishman coming home to Dublin with a hand wrapped in a scarf and explaining that he was treating it carefully 'for this is the hand that shook a hand that shook the world'.

No other fist ever shook the world like John L's. He had, as he himself said, 'a natural ambition for the fighting business', which may or may not be true. But he went through the available boxers in Boston – as well as some unfortunate visitors – like a hot poker through a snowball. By the time he was twenty-one he was a legend – and the word was spreading around New York. There was only one direction when John L was in the ring – forward. He was the real barroom brawler; with a fist as big as many a man's head. He flailed his arms and fists octopus fashion, around every opponent in a tough, even vicious bombardment. He had one motto: 'Hit and hit and hit again until your man goes down or the towel is thrown in.'

When he was setting most opponents running from him in Boston, there was another Irishman, Paddy Ryan, lording the States with the title of Heavyweight Champion. Paddy, born in Tipperary, had won the title in his very first fight, on 30th May 1880. To take the title he beat in the best bare-knuckle style a man who was at the end of his fighting career, Joe Goss. But Goss made Paddy go to eighty-four rounds before he relinquished his title and a thousand dollar sidestake.

This was the man now that Sullivan wanted – and to prove the validity of his claim he took on all comers and promptly beat them. And when Ryan seemed to be ring-shy John L issued a challenge to 'fight any man breathing for any sum from one thousand dollars to ten thousand dollars at catch weights'. And he added that he directed this challenge especially at Paddy Ryan.

But Paddy liked the title and the glory and the money that went with it. He stalled all efforts by Sullivan's backers and would only comment that 'Sullivan is a clever young fellow'. The clever young fellow was building up a fantastic following, both in the ring and out of it. Everywhere he went, the Strong Man from Boston had admiring audiences and it was only a matter of time before public opinion brought the two men face to face. But it didn't happen for almost two years after Ryan won the championship – on 7th February 1882, at Mississippi.

When they stepped into the ring in front of Barnes Hotel, Sullivan, at 196 pounds, was ten pounds lighter and two inches shorter than his opponent – but he was far the more experienced man, doubtlessly fitter and, above all else, he was determined to be heavyweight champion of the world.

According to Sullivan he was in the ring twenty minutes before Ryan put in an appearance and when the champion appeared he was dressed 'in a suit of white drawers and undershirt, flesh coloured stockings and fighting shoes'. Ryan threw an old hat into the enclosure and took his place in the 'north-east corner' accompanied by his manager, seconds, and bottle holders. Sullivan noticed that Ryan 'looked very pale, his old, good-natured smile seeming to have deserted him'.

It wasn't the only thing to desert Ryan that hot spring day. He was on the floor in thirty seconds from a Sullivan right hand – a punch which he himself described later as 'like a telegraph pole had been shoved against me endways'. Round after round went by with Sullivan playing cat and mouse with the champion. In the ninth round the title was changing hands and Ryan, so bruised and battered, was glad to see the end of the affair. In all it had lasted only just over ten minutes.

Now the real life could begin for John L. Back in the opulence of New Orleans there was a lot of celebrating to be got through;

the champagne flowed, the music blared and the most beautiful women in the city lined up to admire the muscles of the new champ. John L was as able for the celebrating as he was for Ryan, and loved it as much as he did winning a fight.

A whole succession of fights followed . . . although few of them were really more than sparring matches for the champ. Whenever he appeared thousands flocked to see him. He toured the country in a variety and athletic combination show, and loved it. The indignity of a knockdown happened once, administered by the English born (Irish parented) Billy Mitchell. John L was so flabbergasted that he swore his legs 'got crossed'. He made up for it by going on to win the fight but was always trying to retrieve his reputation, even going so far as to offer to stand with his hands tied and bet a thousand dollars that Mitchell couldn't knock him out in a dozen tries!

Certainly there was never a man so arrogant in the ring. There was never a man who lived and fought and drank and celebrated in such style as Sullivan. He soaked himself in alcohol, yet still managed to rip apart challengers in a fantastic display of athletic endeavour. The list of the fallen may mean little to even a connoisseur of boxing today but no doubt some of them would have made it had they not met a haymaker from John L on the way. And it wasn't only the boxers who felt the weight of his fist, on one occasion a police chief climbed into the ring to stop a fight and grabbed Sullivan's arm. It was the unwisest effort at arrest that policeman ever made. John L swung and hit him hard on the jaw. But the chief wasn't far enough gone not to blow his whistle and it took the might of a town's police force to hold John L down.

Sullivan managed to get out of this scrape – just as he managed to get out of so many others. His wife never said a bad word about him although he deserted her for a beautiful chorus girl;

the crowds never booed him because he always had a good word for an opponent and few Sullivan fights were complete without a few words from the ringside.

The tone of these speeches was generally in praise of the beaten man. 'He showed a great deal of pluck in standing up to a man of my talent,' John L would doubtfully compliment, 'still I could beat him again, anywhere, any time and with those few remarks I am yours truly, John L Sullivan.'

Yours truly indeed – certainly Boston's truly; and the citizens of his hometown presented him with a belt of solid gold in token of their appreciation. Centrepiece of the belt was a huge eagle-surmounted panel with eight smaller panels showing Sullivan fighting, Sullivan in evening dress, a shield of the United States – and another with an Irish harp. Around this there was a stunning array of almost four hundred diamonds. Everyone knew its value and it became known as 'the ten thousand dollar belt'.

It wasn't just at home that John L was hero – in England the Prince of Wales met him; in France and Australia they turned out in droves to bellow at him. But he was happier in America – it was here that he could earn the money to keep his girlfriend in beautiful clothes and diamonds, to pay for his whiskey gulping, to keep his big round of friends happy. He had one disastrous year in which he was so sick and badly run down that there doesn't seem to have been any disease he didn't have. He was so weak he had to go walking on crutches; he believed he was going to die. But the year after that his manager manged to drag him out of it – and put him in the ring against the mighty Jake Kilrain in the last bare-knuckle championship of the world.

John L at thirty-one was believed to be so badly out of condition that not only Kilrain but the whole crowd got a shock when he stepped into the ring – a tight well-trained 207 pounds against Kilrain's 195. And in this fight John L needed every ounce of strength, and every prayer of his supporters. After forty rounds everyone knew that this was the toughest fight he had ever had; in the forty-fifth he began to vomit and Jake, seeing this, taunted him to 'give it up'.

Taunts meant little to John L. He fought on and on . . . and on. According to all reports the sixty-eighth round was the one that mattered. Sullivan hit Jake with a left to the body and just as the challenger was starting to crumble John L followed up with a right that lifted Kilrain up again . . . and then he went crashing to the ground. Somehow Jake managed to get back on his feet for the next round – and for seven more. But in the seventy-fifth round a sponge was thrown in from Kilrain's corner, and Sullivan had disposed of another challenger. This time it took him two hours and fifteen minutes of intensive fighting in sweltering midday heat.

Two years of idleness followed, during which John L took to the stage. But behind the scenes there was a young man – also of Irish parentage – who was setting a hot pace in affairs of the ring. His name was James J Corbett, Gentleman Jim of later years. Among the highlights of Corbett's early education was a ringside seat, when he was only a teenager, at the Sullivan-Ryan fight and later a sparring match with the great John L himself. It was during this sparring match, which both men conducted – with gloves – at a very gentlemanly pace, that Corbett realised that Sullivan could be beaten by a man who could move and feint – and that man, he was convinced was himself.

But all the time there was the Sullivan boast threateningly hanging over the head of every challenger: 'I can lick any son of a bitch in the world!' And to back up his words he offered a ten thousand dollar challenge to 'any and all the bluffers who have been trying to make capital at my expense'. Included in the challenge was the name of 'James J Corbett of California, who has achieved his share of the bombast'.

So it was Corbett . . . in New Orleans on 7th September 1892. It was a boxing fiesta, three championship fights spread over three days; the first of them going to Irish-born Jack McAuliffe who won the lightweight championship of the world. On the third day came the fight everyone was waiting for. It was hot but just before the fight there was a heavy shower of rain which meant that covers had to be drawn over the arena making the atmosphere hot and damp. It was like a gathering of the tribes of Ireland when the two men crowded with their groups in the corners. There was Casey, Lannon, Moran, McAuliffe, Delaney, Daly, Donovan and Brady dispersing themselves between the two fighters as seconds, managers, coaches, bottle holders etc. There was a thirty-four pound difference in weight, Sullivan, showing a slight softness around the middle, weighing 212 pounds. Corbett was a handsome specimen and magnificently fit, and clever and cunning as well. He started by jeering at Sullivan and taunting him. John L couldn't believe it. Where were all those gentlemanly ways he had been hearing about? And then setting a style that Cassius Clay was to emulate years later he told Sullivan that he had already marked out the round that would see a new champion.

The dancing and prancing of Corbett evaded all the rushes of Sullivan early on and it was the end of round two before a real punch was landed. It came from Corbett to Sullivan's soft middle. The challenger tormented John L with long jabs and all the mighty champion could do was to flail about the empty spaces where any other boxers would have been. For twenty rounds Corbett tantalised and countered and punished and cut Sullivan as the thirty-four-year-old man swayed and clobbered at nothing. In the twenty-first round came a left to the jaw and the mighty John L was down. Twice he tried to rise but the strength was gone, boozed out in quarts and bottles of beer and whiskey.

The crowd roared for the new champion, but they still knew that John L would have something to say. He did – it was all part of the Sullivan tradition. 'Gentlemen,' he said, 'it's part of an old, old story. It's the story of an old man going against a young fellow . . . there are grey hairs in my head . . . I should have known better. I can only say that I'm glad the championship is to stay in America. I remain your warm and personal friend, John L Sullivan.'

He remained a warm and personal friend of the people of America for years after losing his championship. Long after Corbett, Fitzsimmons, James Jeffries, Tommy Burns, Jem Roche, even Jack Johnson failed to draw the crowds, throngs would gather at the mention of the name 'John L Sullivan'. He wined, dined, loved and grew old before his time. Pictures show him round, fat, moustachioed, almost lovable. He died in 1917 soon after a heart attack. He had left his own epitaph: 'I've seen it all. I've lived from A to Z. I've travelled the world and met all kinds of people. But nothing matters any more now. I'm through.'

They held a wake that in true Irish fashion lasted for days. Everyone who was anyone came – Corbett and Kilrain among them. When they took him to bury him the weather was so cold and the ground so hard they had to dynamite his plot. A touch he would have appreciated.

The Irish part in world boxing didn't fade out with Sullivan – there was a steady flow of contenders for all weights, and many a great champion: Dempsey, Sharkey, Flynn, McCarty . . . right down along the weights to other champions in the cut of McAuliffe like the great Rinty Monaghan of recent years. They can all trace their ancestors back to men who wouldn't enjoy a fair or a bazaar if there wasn't a faction fight or a fist fight. There must have been something of the faction fighter in Gene Tunney's Irish father who celebrated his son's birth on 25th May 1897 by going into his local saloon and calling for drinks all round. The reason he gave was good enough for everyone to join with him. 'Today,' he said, ,'a future heavyweight champion of the world was born.' It was the sort of prediction only an Irishman could make – and live to see come true.

PART 5

After the Boyne . . .

CHAPTER I

The Heather Blazing

THE STORY IS told of an incident during the Boer War in which an Irish regiment was reported to 'be making a shift for Ladysmith'.

'Bejasus,' came the Irish reply, 'when they were at home they couldn't even sew on a button.'

Apocryphal, but it summed up in its own way a feeling there was in Ireland at the time, that away from home the Irishman could do just about everything; at home he was far less effective. But then the Irish story on the home ground was a long one of successive disaster and distress – the one real victory between the tenth and twentieth centuries being the victory in 1014 when Brian Boru defeated the Danes at Clontarf just outside – and now well inside – Dublin.

There was a great shough between the Easter of 1014 and the Easter of 1916 in which defeat seemed the only relevant word to the Irish at home. Their fate could be charted with cardio-graphic efficiency – all their battles were fought from the heart but generally ended with a stroke. And in this defeat few nations were as morose as the Irish; the only cure was to get out and leave Ireland to wither in a distillation of tears, poteen and self-pity.

That Good Friday in 1014 should have seen the great resurgence of the Irish. Led by King Brian Boru they beat the Danes into the cold waters of Dublin Bay. It was a day they had been waiting for – but the victory was little more than a curtain raiser for another sad act in the tragedy. Brian was killed by a Danish chieftain as he knelt down to say his prayers after the battle. And where a war should have finished it smouldered again. It stayed in this state of embattled animosity until Diarmuid MacMurrough, as black a rogue as ever walked the land, helped by Henry II, took possession of the country. And that was how in the twelfth century England got a foot in the door that not even the most persuasively waved shillelagh could dislodge for almost eight hundred years.

Even the English had to fight their own battles on Irish soil, first sending Cromwell to massacre his way into the history of the land and kill as many loyal Catholics as he could put to the sword, and then letting James and William range against each other to eventually place the Battle of the Boyne on a bitter pedestal of religion and politics that still survives. It was at the Boyne that William of Orange beat James and set the pattern for Ireland's still raging troubles, placing the Irish Catholics to fight a rearguard action against the king's men, the Protestant Orange Party.

The wars and the killings, the sieges and the oppression, the hypocrisy and the humbug, the men and the treachery, the risings and the rebellions that have spread over the Irish scene since, have filled hearts with wonderment and disbelief.

The rebel-mind was always there but it lost a lot of its power after the Boyne. No longer could a man ride – like Silken Thomas Fitzgerald – through Dublin town accompanied by his own personal cavalry to formally renounce his allegiance to the Crown and go on to declare war on the English. A hundred years before the Boyne this was possible but after it – and until

1793 – no Catholic Irishman could carry a gun, go to University, own a horse worth more than £10, hold even minor office, act as grand juror, take commissions in the army. Small hope then of a population, without natural leaders, ruled by a corrupt government and without ideas, lifting itself to the pinnacle of success.

The hopelessness of it all was so demoralising that the surprising thing is that within a century a leader arose, not from within the peasant class but from Protestant Dublin and with a background of Trinity College. His name was Wolfe Tone who was to scoff at the possibility of death by hanging and disembowelling: 'A fig for the disembowelling if they hang me first.' Somehow Tone took the North and South with all their illogicalities and blended them together; scattering the now inbred timidity with dreams of a revolution as great as that in Paris. The United Irishmen they called themselves and no better title for a group formed in Belfast in those dreary days of 1791 – 'a brotherhood of affection and a communion of rights and a union of power among Irishmen of every religious persuasion'.

Tone carried Ireland into the era of revolution. What had been accomplished in France, what might have been accomplished in England was being attempted in Dublin. In a period wild with oaths ranging from those of the Whiteboys to those of the Peep-o'-day boys there was suddenly a new one for the taking – that of the United Irishmen. Here was a bind on the Irish to emulate the French and take control of their land. The year for the fight for liberty was set for 1798; it was to be a combination Irish rebellion and French invasion. Savage atrocities mixed with brilliant dreams; fantastic plots were devised and simple mistakes brought men to their death; names, often symbols of the orange or the green, mingled and the two fought side by side. But over the whole operation hung a series of great imponderables.

All told, the rebellion was what in modern parlance might be looked at as a fantastic series of happenings – at the rising of the May moon men took their muskets and marched. Led sometimes by priests they presented heroic deeds for historians as they took to the roads and met the yeomen with all their fire. Deaths in that struggle were ferocious, disgusting and barbaric. Irishmen loyal to the Crown were piked to death as part of the public show of strength; and when the pikemen were caught by the yeomen the penalty was just as diabolical. One British soldier, Sergeant Archibald McLaren of the Dunbartonshire Regiment, left behind a diary of the battle showing the extreme cruelty and incredible heroics that marked the rising. McLaren was in Arklow when the Croppies – the insurgents – advanced from victories further south on the town. They appeared 'with their green flags, fixed to poleheads in imitation of colours' and immediately began to fire. Using artillery they had already captured at Gorey they began in real earnest – yet with hindsight their leaders realised that this use of artillery was the worst thing that could have happened. The pikemen were withheld too long; had they been let go there could have been a different result. The pike was a formidable weapon in its day – better in a quick battle than the slow loading and uncertain musket. An attack in time of pikemen could have caused havoc among the military. One insurgent galloped towards the guns:

> One fellow, an officer, galloped in front, having something resembling a stand of colours in his hand, and waving his hat called out 'blood and wounds, my boys, come on, the town is ours'. But ere the foolhardy hero was aware he turned the corner of a house which brought him almost to the mouth of a field piece surrounded by some hundreds of soldiers ready to fire or receive him on the points of their bayonets.

> A volley of small shot sent his horse sprawling in the dust and broke his own thigh; though he fell under his horse he had the cunning enough to lie still and might probably passed for a dead man had he not raised his head to take a peep round him: this being observed, four or five bayonets were plunged into his body. In the midst of his agony he stretched out his arm to shake hands with one of the soldiers but the soldier sent a bullet through his head.

Death was bought easily at Arklow. Father Michael Murphy – one of two Murphy priests, the other was John – met with an end even more terrible. According to the Highlander's diary . . . 'an unmannerly Grape-shot obtruded itself upon his skull before the good man had time to put forth his hand to stop it'. Father Murphy was dragged into a hut which the yeomen promptly set on fire. The Highlander saw the priest next day: 'As I was returning to the barrack my nose was accosted with a disagreeable smell; upon inquiry I found it to proceed from the body of Father Murphy whose leg and thigh were burnt into the very bone. His head was fixed upon the wall of a burnt cabin.' Three days after the battle he saw Father Murphy's head lying in the ditch before the tents.

While Arklow was burning, messages came from all parts of Ireland of other counties rising. Pikes, pitchforks, crucifixes, orange and green mingled in a desperate attempt to bring off the great rebellion. Henry Joy McCracken, Jeremy Hope, Harry Munroe fought their way through the north and there they were accompanied by the storied Betsy Gray who, with her two brothers, rode into battle at Ballynahinch on a white pony wearing a jewelled sword by her side. The Grays were a wealthy family and all involved in the United Irishmen. But one of the great mistakes that seemed to mark the whole rebellion happened to them. Misinterpreting a bugle call which they thought called on them to retire, the three broke and rode away from the battle. They were charged, caught, shot and sabred on the spot. Then, as happened everywhere in this revolt, their bodies were stripped – one soldier taking Betsy's green petticoat and earrings for his wife.

And while the Irish were fighting their way the French were on the sea, but when they landed to help their contribution was small; when they were captured they left the land vowing never to get involved in Ireland's wars again. They 'liked not this land without wine nor discipline where the natives spent their time living on roots, whiskey and lying'.

But while the rebellion moved its slow way through Ireland, the local leaders did not know that in Dublin things were not going as planned. The day before the rising, Lord Edward Fitzgerald, finding himself for a short time leader of the United Irishmen, hid himself away from the hunting Major Sirr. But the good Fitzgerald, always a gentleman, left his boots, militarily labelled, outside his door to be cleaned. He was caught, and died from 'inflammation caused by Major Sirr's pistol wound'.

Disaster piled on top of inexperience and folly; informers were everywhere; there was never any hesitancy on the part of the yeomen to slaughter anyone who got in their way whether they be Croppies or not. Places, people and incidents established themselves for ever in history and song – Boolavogue, Vinegar Hill, Father Murphy, Kelly (the Boy) from Killanne, Shelmelier. Others achieved immortality for inhuman behaviour. One thing was never disputed – the fighting qualities of the men who dreamed of United Ireland. One eye-witness at the battle of Killala reported that the Irish ran 'upon death with as little appearance of reflection or concern as if they were hastening to a show'. But lack of experienced leadership eventually brought disaster and the momentum of the early victories could not be maintained.

Slowly the rising – like the heather – burned itself out. And as it was in its dying flickers, Tone was on the high seas with more French. But his small armada was attacked by British ships and Tone and others were taken prisoner. The French were not mistreated but Tone was to be an example. In November 1798 he was brought to Dublin, court-martialed and sentenced to death. He asked for the death of a soldier: 'Let me be shot by a platoon of grenadiers. I request this indulgence rather in consideration of the uniform which I wear, the uniform of a Chef-de-Brigade in the French Army, than from any personal regard to myself.' But he was ordered to be publicly hanged on 12th November 1798 at 1 pm. Some time in the early hours of the morning he carried out his own plan – when the watch of the guard was relaxed he cut his throat with a penknife blade, partly severing his windpipe. A surgeon was called and closed the wound as best he could. Tone was told that to move his head would be fatal. Preparations for his hanging continued although it seemed unlikely that it would proceed and Sir George Hill was recorded as commenting: 'I would sew up his neck and finish the business.' But while all this was going on, legal efforts were being made to nullify the sentence; a decree of habeas corpus was granted on the grounds that a court martial could not have jurisdiction over civilians except in actual warfare. But the legal bickering went on without the knowledge of Tone's condition. For a week the United Irishman lingered. Once he complained that he was sorry he had been such a bad anatomist. He died on 19th November and was buried in Bodenstown cemetery, a place of honour and pilgrimage still.

On the scaffold which should have taken Tone's life four other United Irishmen died after State trials – the brothers,

Henry and John Sheares, Michael Byrne and John McCann. Others were deported and the number of dead is not recorded, but the Rising of '98 must go down as one of the bloodiest catastrophies of Irish history, and one of the great might-have-beens of world history. While it failed to achieve immediate freedom for the land it laid the foundation stone for independence, it established separatism by pointing the way to an Irish Republic. The man who mournfully told a passing band of insurgents, 'You are a hundred years before your time', wasn't far wrong. Maybe the men marching with their pikes and pitchforks saw it for what it was, the beginning of an ideal, and possibly a beginning to an end of the suggestion that the Irish could fight like heroes anywhere in the world but never at home.

CHAPTER 2

A Sort of Freedom

A THREAD FROM 1798 was carried through the nineteenth century by the Fenians – an organisation which drew more attention than blood in its time but which, nevertheless, crystallised the Irish attitude to the English at long last. 'No matter what government the English offer us it will never be as good as self-government,' they claimed. And the only way to achieve this, they believed, was by violence . . . violence in open rebellion, violence in England, violence against all things British. But like so many other affairs between the two antagonists they won many a battle but failed to win the war.

Their failure in rebellion in 1867 was just another defeat in a series of risings that had been put down in the years since 1798. Basically the Fenians lost because their leadership was not strong enough – a recurring disaster for the Irish at home for generations. They also failed to get all the help they expected from America and finally the Church came out strongly against them. One Kerry bishop spoke for many when he said: 'Hell is not hot enough nor eternity long enough for the punishment' of the Fenian organisers.

The old ways of conspiracy, treachery and chance so evident in Irish life up to this period, played their part in the work and eventual defeat of the Fenians, but before they went they left many scars behind them. In a two-year span they caused explosions in Glasgow, Birmingham, Dublin and in London. Possibly the London ones were the more spectacular – in one day alone they had three 'infernal machines' explode in Westminster Hall, the House of Commons and the Tower of London. They tried, unsuccessfully, to invade Canada – but generally their methods laid the foundations for a new phase of Irish revolutionary history. Above all they wanted to prove that in no way was the Irishman inferior to any other race or creed. They were followed by waves of others – and as the tide came in so the leaders emerged, crowding up in the gallant list of the men of 1916 who died in a battle that reversed all other procedures. This one was lost but the war was won.

Cries from the past from the pikemen of Wexford who were jeered as 'Ireland's toy soldiers' carried the slow-burning fuse into Dublin's heart on Easter Monday, 1916, when less than two thousand men rose and fought the most glorious rising in Irish history, a fight that finally wiped away the cynical suggestion that the Irishman could never fight at home. It is a long roll-call – Pearse, Connolly, MacDonagh, MacDiarmada, Ceannt, Plunkett, Houston, O'Hanrahan, Daly, Colbert, all died in front of British firing squads in a week-long orgy of vengeance that did nothing to improve the image of 'the invaders'.

The Rising of 1916 threw up many heroes as well as martyrs – de Valera, Collins, Griffith, Cosgrave and many others, who, living through the battle and subsequent Civil War, went on to lead Ireland through turbulent years of politics. But the fighting Irishman, the impetuous, mercurial, ebullient, violent, rampaging, courageous soldier, was epitomised in one man whose name is hardly known outside Ireland. His name was Cathal Brugha, a far more romantic designation than the anglicised form of mere Charles Burgess. His wild heroics will be filtered from the book of 1916 whenever anyone happens to be looking for a man in the mould of the Irishmen who strode through the continental wars of the seventeenth and eighteenth centuries, and even against these the Cathal Brugha story will read more like fiction than the fact it is.

Dublin on that Easter in April 1916 was an extraordinary place. Here was a rising taking place right under the very nose of the British garrison and in the very heart of the city. The rebels gathered at Liberty Hall and marched away to their destinations – bakeries, breweries, hotels, hospitals, anywhere that looked a good vantage point in the city. The main group marched to the General Post Office, suicidally in the centre of Dublin's main street. They cut all communications and ran up their own flag – green with a golden harp and with the Gaelic lettering 'Irish Republic' across it. They issued a proclamation and waited for the real fight to begin.

Much the same sort of activity was going on in other places throughout the city. The Royal Dublin Union near the banks of the Grand Canal was just one of these. Here a total of forty-three officers and men set out to hold a huge, rambling building of old people's maternity and general hospital wards. To do this they had to split up into relatively small groups. Among the insurgents were Cathal Brugha, the Vice-Commandant, and Lieutenant William Cosgrave, later to become President of the Irish Free State. A force of some fifty British soldiers, very ably led, was sent in to take the rebel garrison. But they went in without the ferocity of Brugha on their side.

As the fighting in the Union spread throughout the wards and lobby, both the rebels and the army got inflated ideas of the other's strength. The insurgents believed that a force of some thousands was holding them down while the British were told that some hundreds of rebels had taken command of the place. It was a classic situation for panic and courage. In one extraordinary moment a man named Joyce, engrossed in holding his position, suddenly noticed that things around him had gone quiet. He looked around and found he was holding a position alone. He hadn't heard the order to retreat.

Brugha, second last down the stairs, reached the bottom just as a bomb was thrown by a British soldier. As it burst into fragments he was hit in several places; then rifle shots raked the area, at least one bullet ripping into Brugha. But somehow he managed to pull himself, badly wounded into the shelter of a kitchen doorway. There he turned himself on to his stomach and pointed his heavy rifle towards the area where he expected the British. Footsteps echoed and into sight trundled the last man of the company.

'God, what happened to you,' gasped Joyce at the sight of Brugha lying badly bleeding on the floor.

'Nothing,' replied the Vice-Commandant, 'they've gone.'

Joyce was worried about the officer's condition, but he was told not to worry, just to look after himself. Then Brugha took a watch from his pocket and asked Joyce to see that it was given to his wife, after that he asked for a glass of water. Just as he got the water there was a cry from the other side of the lobby. 'Surrender' came the British call . . . but the only answer was a volley from Brugha's rifle. He told Joyce to get away and to tell the others that he would hold the position as long as he could.

Dashing away to the rest of the battalion Joyce found their spirits very low, but they were adamant that they would fight to the last man. They recited a decade of the rosary and as they finished they heard a voice singing 'God Save Ireland'. No one could guess who it was, Joyce's report of Brugha's condition had been more than gloomy. But when a man ventured out to see where the singing was coming from, he saw to his amazement the figure of Brugha who had pulled himself from the kitchen into an adjacent yard and was now propped up against a wall, with a good view of the barricade. Every now and then he loosed a few shots at it as if to dare the military to charge over it. His singing was defiant and in between choruses he challenged the soldiers to come and fight. The weak, bleeding figure roused his comrades: renewed, they rushed from their rooms and took command of the barricade. The military fell back, out of the Union, the insurgents held them there, thanks to Brugha. But by now communications between the various outposts of the Rising were rapidly disintegrating, no one was sure what was going on, and the group dispersed to fight in other positions.

When the inevitable surrender came, 1351 people had been killed or severely wounded. No doubt Brugha was included in this total and certainly the British considered him too far gone to worry about. He had enough wounds for six men and he was carried into the Union a dying man. But the guts that had shown themselves in his one-man stand came to his aid again. He fought death and won, one of the few to escape the orgy of revenge, and lived to plunge himself right into the middle of the inevitable Civil War that razed Ireland again in 1922. How he ever managed it became one of the mysteries of Dublin. Everywhere he went people swore that the bullets and fragments of bombs still embedded in him 'rattled and jingled'.

The part-freedom offered by England to Ireland in the years after 1916 was not the sort of freedom that Brugha and many Republicans wanted for their land. They would settle for nothing less than absolute, but there were men who were willing to settle for something – they did and the Irish Free State was born. It was almost stillborn. There to willingly accept only what they wanted were the Republicans, led by de Valera with Brugha, a man never out of the reckoning. On the other side was William

Cosgrave, who had been in the Union with Brugha, and that other folk-hero Michael Collins. The Civil War inevitably followed throwing the land into chaos again.

Cathal Brugha faced the National Army in O'Connell Street in the early days of July, 1922, after days of skirmishes in the capital. On the opposite side to the General Post Office and further north in the street was the block that is now the Gresham Hotel. In this block Brugha and a small garrison of Republicans held out against the Free State troops. Restlessly, like one caged Brugha patrolled the rooftops of the block. In his hand was a Mauser automatic on to which he had fitted a rifle butt. He was domineering, alert and overlorded the garrison of some thirty women and seventy men. With him in the building were other leading Republicans, Austin Stack and Oscar Traynor, as well as the man who was regarded as the leader, de Valera. They held on for some time, relentlessly crossing fire with the National Troops who were using every tactic open to men with the freedom of the street. Pressure became intense and it was decided to withdraw from the block. Quietly and mysteriously most of the men filtered away – despite the cordon of National troops around the building – but Brugha and a few remained.

Brugha had what most of the other men around did not have – a personal knowledge of how to handle a close situation like this one. Memories of the old Union days when he fought the British, must have flooded his mind – only this time the men opposite were once old buddies. Now they were mortal enemies. So much did Brugha's astonishing courage worry the National troops that they made a request to the British Government for a supply of gas to help them rid O'Connell Street of the now diminishing garrison. While the British hesitated, the National troops pounded the building with all sorts of fire – from small arms to an eighteen-pounder. Machine guns cut the air with a deadly hiss and soon the main building was ablaze. The building was soon on fire from end to end; the Republicans were now trapped in small groups of twos and threes. Those who couldn't escape or didn't die in the holocaust surrendered. But still there were a few who wouldn't give in. As the whole building tumbled in a shower of smoke and flames, two days after the first flames, the nerveless Brugha remained with full control of the small group of wounded and undaunted men.

Brugha's control is shown in a story told by Cal Younger in *Ireland's Civil War*. Soon after the main building collapsed a white flag went up from the roof close by. To the National troops it was a flag of truce – but not to Brugha. He was waving it to tell the Army that the firemen who were fighting the flames nearby were in danger of being blown up by mines – an action of extraordinary thoughtfulness at such a moment of crisis.

But the flames from the main building soon gulped their way to the spot where Brugha and the small group were still determinedly holding on. Now there was nothing for it. The women and the medical orderlies were sent out. Then as if in warning a chemical store at the rear burst into flames. Surrender was the only way out. Led by Art O'Connor the remnants of the garrison made their way out not knowing that Burgha had no intention of accompanying them. They were out in the street when the realisation hit them; the National Army officers realised it as well. But they didn't reckon on the blazing exit of Burgha from the building. As the flames flickered all around him he burst from the door, his gun spewing bullets all around him. The almost stunned soldiers facing him were saved from death by a Lewis gunner stationed on the corner of a nearby building. He opened up and Brugha crumpled on the street.

His death in hospital a few days later was inevitable, it was so much in the tradition of Wolfe Tone and the men who died in

1916. It was heroics on a grand scale at a time when heroes were killed every day. Brugha's sacrifice did not go unheeded: even the Free Staters, when offering prayers for their own dead heroes, had a Mass said for the repose of the soul of Cathal Brugha, which in itself was an extraordinary reaction. Extraordinary – for in Ireland old hatreds die hard.

CHAPTER 3

The IRA

The civil war settled very little; it left unattained its main target – the creation of one whole and undivided Ireland. There had been so much bloodshed that the majority were glad to settle for twenty-six of the thirty-two counties – but not all. There, in full idealism, was the IRA ready to fight and die to unite Ireland; to make it a land where green and orange could live in harmony. No other name in the past half century has been liable to put such fear or favour into Irish hearts as the IRA. For almost fifty years this now illegal organisation has been part of the Irish scene – regarded by some as the Robin Hoods of Irish patriotism and taking only a minute part of what is owed to their nation; regarded by others as a daily threat to a way of life.

The Irish Republican Army follows in a long tradition of Irish 'illegal' organisations on a bitter treadmill of violence. In various phases of Irish history there have been Steel Boys, Whiteboys, Oak Boys, Peep-o'-day boys, and many others, dedicated to keeping the land either all green or all orange. None of them have stayed so firmly in the public eye as the IRA who prove, if proof was needed, that the savage laws of history die a slow death in Ireland.

No one really knows the full strength of the IRA. In 1970

reports varied from 'two thousand men ready and willing to fight' to a 'mere skeleton' of a group. One of their leaders said: 'Now they say the IRA has only two hundred men but when they want to scare people they say two thousand. The IRA has grown as big as it wants to grow. There have been volunteers greater than the need of or the capacity to absorb them. The IRA can be very selective now in who they take in.'

Most of the men who head the IRA are battle-hardened veterans who took part in the 1939 bombing campaign in England or in the more recent major violent campaign along the Irish border in 1956–61. They are determined to continue their fight to clear Ireland of all British influence. They are backed by a rank and file membership that is little different from any army. There is no coercion in their methods of recruitment and a man may leave at any time – all he is expected to do is to keep his mouth shut and reveal nothing that will in any way endanger anyone still in the group. They have arms – the most modern machine guns and small arms – and a degree of intimacy with explosives that is nothing short of expert. Most of the armaments come through the normal international dealer organisations, but if this fails there is generally enough 'loose English hardware' available for a competent commando group to pick up, as in the raid carried out in Northern Ireland at the start of the campaign of the 1950s. This campaign showed the lengths to which the IRA was prepared to go when the chips were down and anyone who, even with hindsight, relegates it to the status of a Gilbertian farce, should remember that there is no joke where men are prepared to die.

Take the place, the time and the plan for the raid in Armagh in 1954.

The Place:	Gough Barracks. A grey British Army garrison sheltering behind high walls and iron gates in the song-famed city of Armagh, just over the border in Ulster.
The Time:	2.40 pm. A warm, sunny Saturday afternoon in June. The streets of the city bustle with weekend shoppers. In the barracks there is little activity.
The Plan:	One of the most daring and brazen daylight commando raids ever carried by the IRA.

A large, enclosed, red cattle truck pulls up close to the barrack gates. A man hops out and loudly thanks the driver for the lift. He walks to the barracks gate and speaks to the sentry.

'How does a fella go about joining the Army, mate?' he asks.

'On a Saturday?' queries the sentry.

'I don't care whether it's a Saturday or a Sunday,' replies the man.

'Well, I think you're a bloody fool to want to join the Army, now or anytime. Hang on and I'll ask the corporal of the guard to see you.'

He whistles shrilly and the corporal and another soldier come out of the guardroom. As they do three other men, dressed in British Army uniforms, walk from the back of the truck and go into the guardroom, ignoring the talk at the gate. A fourth follows them and joins the gathering at the gate.

'What can I do for you?' asks the corporal.

'Stand still. Act natural and I won't have to kill you,' replies the prospective recruit.

The corporal looks down into the barrel of a Colt .45 and laughs. It can only be a joke.

'It's no joke,' snaps the man. 'If you think it is look over your shoulder.' The corporal and the two legitimate soldiers look towards the guardroom door. A Thomson sub-machine gun is pointing at them.

'Move into the guardroom and do it naturally,' orders the man. 'It's an IRA raid.'

The group move into the guardroom where the rest of the guard stare unbelievingly at an array of revolvers and machine guns. The telephone is put out of order; one of the soldiers is told to strip; then they are all tied up. The man who a minute before wanted to join the army makes the uniform of the stripped soldier fit him. He takes the sentry's place at the gate.

The lorry is now signalled to enter. It drives straight through, past the guardroom and up to the armoury. Five men dressed in British Army battledress jump from the back of it, walk into the building and overpower the guards. They begin loading the lorry with arms and ammunition; a Bren gun is held back, cocked and ready for duty.

Opposite the armoury is a block of married quarters. Some women watch the guns being loaded. A civilian approaches the IRA men. He wants to know where they are taking the arms.

'You'd better ask the officer in charge,' says one of the raiders and directs the man into the armoury. There he is bound and gagged with the two soldiers. A lorry load of weekend soldiers arrives and, as it goes past, the part-timers wave to the IRA men who wave back.

A regular stream of men and officers arrive at the guardroom. They are all sent inside by the sentry. And once inside they too are bound and gagged.

Less than fifteen minutes have gone now since the operation started.

Suddenly a woman in the married quarters spots something strange. One of the IRA men has saluted a passing officer – with his left hand! Quickly she realises that there is something wrong.

She shouts to a man who runs to the guardroom to call out the guard. But once inside the guardroom he joins the growing group of bound and gagged men. The woman tries to phone. But the telephone is out of order. She runs to a friend's house and calls the local police station. Almost incoherently she shouts: 'They're loading up arms and ammunition here at Gough Barracks. Something's gone wrong!'

The policeman pacifies her. Yes, they'll send someone around. She shouldn't get so excited. Then the 'phone is hung up. But she still isn't satisfied. She calls to a lorry driver and tells him her fears He sees the men loading the red truck. He drives his lorry to the main gate and tries to block the gateway.

The IRA sentry's gun points at him.

'Back the truck or I'll kill you.'

The driver tries to jump out the other side but another IRA man is there with a revolver in his hand. 'Move it. And don't be so silly as to try anything.' The driver moves the lorry, gets down and is taken to the guardroom.

Two other soldiers spot the danger. They try to scale the wall into the street but IRA men are covering them. They drop back into the barrack square and are bundled into the now crowded guardroom.

Twenty minutes have now gone.

The lorry is well loaded. The order is given to clear out. Everyone takes his place, quietly and efficiently in the lorry and the red intruder slips out into the busy Saturday afternoon streets of Armagh.

Twenty minutes after the woman's 'phone call a lone policeman answers the frantic telephone call. He arrives on a bicycle . . .

No trace is ever found of the arms. No one knows where the lorry can have 'disappeared' to. The haul, which according to a British Army officer was 'brilliantly planned', was made up of rifles, revolvers, Sten guns, Bren guns, Thomson sub-machine guns and a lot of ammunition.

This classic commando raid – which with typical Irish fondness for euphemism was called an incident – switched the spotlight back on the Irish Republican Army. It was a spotlight that had flickered occasionally through the years since the 1920s when the departing British divided Ireland in two. Twenty-six counties, mainly Catholic, became known as the Irish Free State (later Irish Republic), while six north-eastern counties called Northern Ireland and mainly Protestant, stayed loyal to the British crown. Since that agreement there have always been Irishmen ready to fight for 'the freedom of all-Ireland'.

This willingness was not widely approved of in the Irish Republic – and even less so in Northern Ireland. One editor said: 'paramilitary histrionics of the IRA annoy, bewilder and sadden a great majority of Irish people. That the name "Irish Republican Army" is used not only causes annoyance but it usurps the title of Ireland's legitimate army.'

The Armagh raid was so impudently accomplished that it was exactly what the IRA needed to keep the cause alive and to bring in new, young recruits. It was the big revival point of the 'fifties. It brought men, and the arms to train them, for what IRA men call 'our 1956 campaign'.

This campaign lasted well into 1962 and overjoyed the hard core of all-or-nothing Republicans.

Headlines after the raid, in the IRA backed monthly newspaper, the *United Irishman*, shouted out praise.

'Well done, lads.'

'Arms will be used against British forces.'

'Get England out.'

'A Tonic.'

And on a lighter note new lyrics were published for 'The Homing Waltz'. The last lines went:

We found what we prayed for
The arms we were made for
That day in Gough Barracks in County Armagh.

And with the revival of interest, money started to come to the IRA. Most of it came from America where over-romantic Irish-Americans have nourished Irish republicanism since the days when the first banknotes were printed in the US for a Fenian government that never materialised.

No doubt it was US money that kept the IRA alive. The organisation was very much the playtoy of sentimental Irish Americans about this time. The subscription list in any copy of the *United Irishman* shows just where the money came from. These two examples were taken from random issues of the paper in the 1950s.

> *USA* – San Francisco $400; J Stankard $5; Local 147 Compressed Air Workers Union $325; New York branch $700.

And from another issue:

> *USA* – Donegal Men's Assoc per New York branch $100; Mrs Daly, Chicago $5; Tim Keyes, Brooklyn, $3; New York branch $400; Mrs Williams, New York, $5; P Clifford, Conn, $10; Peter Toal, Bronx $5.

All through the files there will be found references to funds from America. 'Of course we depend on money from America,' said a member of the paper's staff as he talked in the dim, poorly furnished office in a big Dublin Georgian house. 'We are no different from a lot of other people and organisations in Ireland.'

From a conversation with any member of the organisation it could be seen that it is American money that kept alive the vendetta against all things British. 'It finances violent young men, assisted by some superannuated militarists, to perpetuate bitterness in the belief that they are helping to end it,' said an editorial in one of Ireland's daily newspapers at the time.

But not only US money was involved. Arms have been smuggled into the country by returning emigrants. One man who didn't get his quota through was stopped as he disembarked from the liner *Ryndam* from New York. The man had been working as a clerk in the Bronx. Customs men, going through his luggage, opened a compartment of a wardrobe-type trunk and found, covered by clothing, two submachine guns, six revolvers, a rifle and 470 rounds of ammunition.

Of course there were other sources of arms supply. Two soldiers of the Irish Army admitted stealing twenty-nine revolvers, a hundred thunderflashes and a large quantity of ammunition from a store on their camp. They stole it 'for the fight in the north'.

It wasn't so much a fight that was carried into the north. More a series of 'incidents' which did nothing to heal the forty-year-old festering sore.

Vaults seldom used in Armagh's Cathedral were used to hide stolen guns – unknown to the clergy. The Cathedral was also used as the hiding-place for three men who were captured in the confessional box by a policeman who followed them.

Bridges were blown up, trains derailed, customs posts wrecked.

But the arms game brought a violent death for five young men before one raid at the foot of the Mountains of Mourne. A still unexplained explosion in the hillside cottage where they were assembling was of such force that it blew the tops off trees and threw parts of the cottage two hundred yards away. Four of the men were IRA volunteers, the fifth the owner of the cottage. All died horribly, a surgeon recording that two of them died as a result of complete body disintegration. Today a memorial erected by the IRA marks the site of the cottage.

'Some vainglorious young fools,' was the description given by a Dublin newspaper to the raiders who held up a train that turned out to be an excursion special for laundry workers from Dublin. On this occasion the raiders were wearing full British battledress, soot on their faces, and yellow and gold flashes on their sleeves.

'The childishness of the minds behind this kind of thing would seem to be comic if it were not also terrifying,' said an editorial. 'Grown-up children are a menace to the society in which they live. They believe they are fighting for a just and holy cause. There is no sharp intelligence behind them . . .'

However, there was little of a child's game about the raids that shocked the world on New Year's eve, 1956, and the following New Year's Day:

> New Year's Eve. The village of Derrylin is quiet. Most of the villagers are in the community hall at a concert. No one sees the forty well-armed men with blackened faces and wearing a miscellany of uniforms, slide into the dense undergrowth and move up behind the tall trees that screen the heavily sandbagged police station. Extra precautions have been taken at the police station. A few days before, a raid was beaten off by the eight men manning the post – but no one expects another raid so quickly. The policemen sit around a big turf fire, unsuspecting.
>
> Suddenly the letterbox in the heavily barred and bolted door bursts open. The muzzle of a revolver is pushed through and the first shot is fired.
>
> The bullet from the revolver zips death with it. Constable Scally, a twenty-three-year-old member of the Royal Ulster Constabulary, lurches forward from his chair by the fire.

Before he can be taken to hospital later that night he is dead.

A bomb wrecks the front door. Grenades are thrown in. Glass smashes. Revolvers crack. Explosions shatter the building. And when the fire is returned by the police the raiders slip away.

A heavy guard is placed on the border. Yet through this tight-meshed net another band of raiders slip the following night.

This time the force in only ten strong. They drive in an open lorry up to the police station at Brookborough, seat of the then Prime Minister of Northern Ireland, Lord Brookborough, and not far from Derrylin.

This raid is destined to produce the kind of hero the IRA badly needs at this time, political martyrs. Quickly the men place mines around the police station but before they can be exploded the raiders are spotted. Police, up to 1970, always armed in Northern Ireland, are quickly in action. They take up positions behind slotted windows, searchlights are played around the area, and the raiders' fire is returned.

Seated on the back of an open lorry, firing a machine gun, is the rebels' section leader, a handsome, spectacled, fair-haired Irish scholar of twenty-eight, Sean South. He has no protection, is hit and dies instantly. Near him a teenage boy, named Fergal O'Hanlon, writhes in pain as bullets rip through his legs and thighs. The lorry drives off at top speed but soon runs out of petrol. The raiders retire to a cowshed; South's body is left there, so too is the now unconscious O'Hanlon.

The rest of the party – four of them badly wounded – head away over the rocky, boggy mist-shrouded Slieve Beagh (the Little Mountain). They dump their arms, scatter and get away.

When the report of the raid comes through O'Hanlon too is dead – found beside the body of South.

The two dead men are now heroes and martyrs. Today there is seldom a ballad concert where a song commemorating their exploits is not sung. Two of the most popular are 'Sean South of Garryowne' and the Dominic Behan composition about the dead O'Hanlon 'The Patriot Game'. In the suburbs of Dublin a luxurious modern estate is called South Park in memory of the dead Sean.

But these raids and deaths achieved nothing. They only reopened old wounds in a country where there is no feud like an old feud and where tempers and passions are fierce. More than ever they divided Ireland against itself.

A dangerous backlash soon became evident. Police became jittery and trigger-happy and many completely innocent people fell victims. Tip-offs that led to police raids became an everyday hazard for Catholic families in the Protestant dominated North. It opened new avenues for retaliation in personal feuds among neighbours. One mother had the anguish of seeing her five sons taken off to prison after police found guns and ammunition on their farm. She swore they knew nothing of the arms and that someone who wanted to do them harm had planted them. In many cases the arms were later found to be planted, although the innocent people were in prison.

And the IRA raids went on, aiming at the dream that had been nurtured through centuries.

Always behind these raids was the principle that a thirty-two-county Ireland was a natural unit. And the belief that the only way this could be achieved was by force. But after six bloody and frightening years the IRA called a halt to these adventures. Their 'peace' statement, while acclaimed throughout the world, was not a withdrawal of the principle of armed aggression which many people thought it was.

The statement gave an account of the campaign. It said that six hundred raids had taken place in Northern Ireland, six of the Northern Ireland security forces had been killed, twenty-eight wounded. Two of their own organisation had been killed in action, seven accidently, an organiser shot dead and a small number wounded. Forty-three members were serving sentences from five to fifteen years in Belfast jail; three in England and forty-two in Dublin where the organisation is just as illegal as it is in the North.

Statistical statements of this kind are available to anyone who visits the offices of the *United Irishman* or any one of the five organisations involved in 'the cause' –

SINN FEIN (the political organisation)
FIANNA EIREANN (a boy scout type group which, it is claimed, is *NOT* a recruiting group for the IRA)
CUMANN NA MBAN (the female group which is not very strong)
CUMANN NA GCAILINI (girl guide equivalent)
And, of course, the IRA.

But it is impossible to get any reliable guide to the numbers actively involved in these organisations. Training camps are a good guide to establishing the strength of the IRA. But, because they are illegal, meetings are held in out-of-the-way mountain areas. Some of these camps have been disturbed by the police and arrests – up to as many as thirty men – have been made. Countrywide round-ups, too, of known IRA men have brought seventy arrests in one night at the height of the activity. Numbers now are certainly decreasing, and it is believed that the *United Irishman*, once with a circulation of over 120,000, dipped to a publishing figure of 30,000. Sinn Fein, once strong politically, were down to four seats in the Irish Dail (parliament) in 1960 and then lost them. In the recent elections no Sinn Fein candidate was even put forward.

It was this obvious weakness of the IRA that brought about the cessation of activities in 1962. Time was needed to reorganise, 'to augment resources and prepare for a more favourable situation,' said one member.

For over a year little was heard of the IRA and obviously a show of strength was needed by the organisation if they were to get new recruits and more funds. But nothing as sensational as the famous Armagh raid was forthcoming. Instead, indignation at the visit of England's Princess Margaret whose husband, Lord Snowdon, came to visit his mother in Ireland, sparked off more 'incidents'.

Bombs were exploded, trees cut to block roadways, normally dormant little country towns were torn asunder with rioting, a police car was overturned. The various appearances in court that followed the riot gave the IRA scope for dramatics and one judge who tried the men was abused as he left the courtroom.

But little or nothing came to the IRA from these activities. Again it only served to bring down the wrath of Irish newspapers on their heads and there was little sign of any great revival in the organisation. But to show they were still a force to be reckoned with, a group allowed a British television unit to film 'freedom fighters' training for the next campaign.

These fighters were generally mostly very young idealists. 'They are fastidious even to the point of fanaticism,' said one paper, 'about small things . . .' The 'small things' include a general dislike of swearing, drinking, and the English language. In all, they are a very different type of IRA men to the wild boys like Brendan Behan, who dominated the organisation in the

1940s. Behan, who drank with the best of them, saw the new type of IRA coming and it didn't please him. His approach to the IRA was summed up in a far less idealistic way than any of the next generation would agree with. 'If the big powers like America and Russia can drop their big bombs surely the IRA are entitled to drop little ones.'

But while Brendan backed the IRA with words, his own place in the organisation is uncertain. 'The IRA had the good military sense never to make me more than a messenger,' he once said – but he did serve his share of time in prison for his allegiance. Caught carrying explosives in Liverpool (his grandmother was once jailed on a similar charge), Brendan was in Borstal for eighteen months. Back in Ireland, after his release, he wasn't long out of trouble and was sentenced to fourteen years for shooting at a policeman. He served four before he was released under a general amnesty, but it wasn't long before he was back under the roof of another jail – British this time – for helping an IRA man to escape from the police.

On this occasion a compatriot was to be 'rescued' from Leyhill Prison in Surrey and it was Brendan's job after the 'rescue' to guard a Park Ranger in the vicinity of the prison. 'A decent man,' Brendan recounted,' a quiet respectable Irishman he was who, even though he was employed by the British Imperial Majesty, never spoke a word against us or his native country. Helpful . . . never a bit of trouble. And the only effin thing I did to convince him of our good intentions was to hold a .45 revolver to his head all the time. Cocked.' The operation was a success – for all but Brendan. He was caught and lived up to his own description as 'the most captured soldier in Irish history'.

Other IRA men spent longer terms in prison than Brendan – mostly in England. They say they prefer English jails and certainly some of the stories they tell about Irish 'concentration' camps justify their choice. Usually, however, they don't talk about their imprisonments. 'When you've been through it once, it doesn't matter,' they say. And after that they say little. It is, generally speaking, a matter of 'you mind your business, I'll mind mine.'

Never accuse an I.R.A. man of "playing soldiers". There was a time when you might have been laughed at . . . not now. It is a serious role, far from the game of soldiers. It was before the 1969 confrontation that I was talking about this subject with some of the younger members of the I.R.A. in their Gardiner Place headquarters. They were wearing green battledress tunics and peaked caps (bought, they said, in a Dublin supermarket for less than £1.) But they wouldn't agree it was a uniform. Their idealism didn't need a uniform, they said. And what about their force . . . was it aiming at a r evolution? Their reply was that every country had to have a force of rebellion ("After us will come the real soldiers, the people . . . we are the image makers.") Historically they have many heroes, mostly from Ireland's past, but when pressed to name the man they admire most in the world today they agree it's Castro.

'Even if he is a Communist you have to admire what he has done for the Cuban people,' they said. 'He had only a handful of men, like us, at one time and yet he liberated his country. Every country needs leaders. We are the leaders of Ireland. Through us the country will be liberated.'

They laughed at the suggestion that the problem of partition would ever be solved by peaceful means alone.

'Never a chance. Anyway, the people expect fight from us,' said one teenager. 'If you don't take action they call you yellow-bellied and when you do they call you a terrorist and a criminal.'

They reiterated strongly that their main object in life – was to see the north 'freed'. They would not acknowledge that within four years they were unlikely to be members of the IRA. Four years is regarded as the span of active interest of an IRA man.

The strange thing about the IRA is the ease with which it has seemed through the years to slip in and out of these valleys of inactivity. There was a strange lapse during the 1969 troubles in Northern Ireland when the IRA issued, and then withdrew, orders to join in the fight. Their eventual aim, said a leader, was to work to 'a disciplined strategy'. This strategy was, he claimed, only aimed at helping people badly in need in Belfast and not to join in the fight.

But it was an uneasy silence . . . and an uneasy position. Few people could see the IRA in a defensive, even peacekeeping, role in the troubles. Certainly the Protestants couldn't, and set up their own retaliatory fighting unit, the Ulster Volunteer Force. But the IRA meant it. Head down they waited, but one young man, a university student, summed it up: 'There is a Byronic romanticism about Ireland's patriots that is indestructible . . . this is only a lull.'

CHAPTER 4

The Next Tragedy . . .

AND A LULL it was – a lull between a period of aggravation and an all-out guerrilla war. The long-held dream of a united Ireland was still held strongly by the IRA and this, coupled with a despairing poverty in the ghettos of Belfast and in the slums of Derry, caused an explosion of frightening force in a corner of the country where more relevance was placed on events of three hundred years ago than on the needs of the twentieth century. No one really expected that such a ferocious cauldron was going to be exposed, bubbling with hatred, despair, desolation and the malice of centuries; no one really expected that this festering antagonism was going to fill in another chapter, more tragic than any other, of the story of the fighting Irish.

Why did it happen? The answer is easy – because of the carelessness and complacency of governments and politicians of both orange and green. Certainly the failure to establish a state where the norms of democracy were seen to be adhered to; failure to create a system that was as kind to one man as to another, that was as stern with one man as another, were the kernel of the trouble. Indeed, with hindsight it seems that most governments of the six north-east counties only served to keep alive the old fires of bitterness. But not all the blame can rest in Belfast. Through the years there had been an almost complete lack of foresight by those in authority in Dublin and London as well. Politicians – by omission – were leaving another mess that could only be cleaned by blood.

When the lull came to an end is easy to date. It was on 12th August 1969, in the old city of Derry (the name you give it if you're a Republican) or Londonderry (if you're not). On that day the double talk and the double standards of government swept Northern Ireland up in a wave of savagery, rioting, burnings, killings, killings and more killings. The tameless violence of that day put this small corner of Ireland on a plateau that surpassed Cyprus, Aden, Algeria and, at times, even Vietnam. This last analogy might be scorned at but in truth in one week in 1969 – to be repeated in 1971 – more people were killed in this Irish conflict than in the Vietnam fighting.

On that 12th August the Irish paraded with fife, drum and gun into the headlines of the world. It was an anniversary march, one of the many that rouse tempers in Northern Ireland, celebrating the fifteen week siege of the city in 1689 when Protestants held out against James II's army. On that day, thirteen apprentice boys shut the gates of the city against troops sent to garrison Derry by the king. The apprentice boys established a place for themselves in Irish history and are still very much part of the Orange tradition. Today's Apprentice Boys make up a very strong section of the Protestant community who march each year, not only to celebrate but to prove to the Roman Catholic majority in the city that the Protestant is still in ascendancy.

The bands played traditional Orange tunes as they marched through the streets bedecked with Union Jacks and red, white and blue bunting. The world expected a confrontation of some sort; it had been building up in bouts of bad temper between the two factions for some time and a call to have the parade banned was ignored by the Government of Northern Ireland. It wasn't, they felt, really necessary . . .

It began with some jeers, then stones were thrown. The marching Apprentice Boys protected themselves as best they could: soon they were returning the Catholic missiles. The Royal Ulster Constabulary, never loved by the Catholic community in the North, were prepared – riot equipment, helmets and shields were donned and batons drawn. The police charged the crowds, and the match was set to an inflammable situation. Before the night was over houses, factories, lorries, cars, barricades burned and exploded. In the morning ninety-four policemen were injured and thirteen were still in hospital. There were, according to statistics, fewer civilians injured but this didn't take into account the numbers who were treated when the Bogsiders set up their own medical treatment unit in their area.

This Derry confrontation laid bare the whole hating heart of the North. In a mood of violent retaliation a mob moved out into the streets of Belfast intent on first levelling the score with the Catholics and then putting themselves firmly back in control. The Catholic areas were caught undefended. There was no IRA – a while before, the organisation had said they believed in a campaign of non-violence, a campaign that looked, at first, to be working effectively. Promises had been made by the British and Northern Ireland Governments that all reforms demanded by the Catholic community would not only be done but be seen to be done. Now that whole situation was being reversed, and the mob roamed at will, burning and threatening. It has been said, and there seems little reason to doubt it, that the whole Catholic area of the Falls in Belfast would have been razed in those following days. There were seemingly no defenders, until a handful of men realised that on them the whole fate of the Catholic community rested. They weren't far-seeing politicians, they weren't community leaders, they were ex-IRA men who had opted out of the fighting in favour of younger men many years before. But the situation was desperate. With a tommy-gun, hoarded against the day it might be needed, and a few small arms this group of six or seven men went into action against a free roving and shooting mob. Fêted as saviours they are still heroes in the Falls area of Belfast today.

That was how it began; it wasn't the first time the pogrom had come into the life of Belfast. Other times and others years had seen violent religious clashes but this time it had all the look of a situation that could only end in civil war.

The escalation was dramatic . . . Irish troops moved to border line . . . refugee camps were set up south of the border . . . the notorious B-Specials, an armed extra police force, feared and hated for long by Catholics, was disbanded . . . the Royal Ulster Constabulary was disarmed . . . British troops were drafted to the North in ever increasing numbers. New personalities developed, some to be lost in the grey smoke of CS gas that came to be a daily part of the Irish air.

There was – and is – the Rev Ian Paisley ('Thank God I'm a menace to Popery'), vociferous and hating and often called the greatest Irish politician for years.

There was – and is – Bernadette Devlin ('I'm not against force'), vociferous and hating and often called the greatest Irish politician for years.

There was – once – a man called Major Bunting, Paisley's commander-in-chief who just disappeared from the scene and watched the confrontation, not from the front line, but from his front window.

There was – once – Eddie McAteer, leader of the Republicans who suffered too because when it came to the crunch he was out of touch.

On the Catholic side new leaders arose: John Hume, a young married man from the heart of the troubled Derry city, the Bogside; Ivan Cooper, a Protestant who was involved first in Civil Rights but who soon became active to a great degree in the whole cause of the repressed minority of the north. There were others on this side: Gerry Fitt, from the tough Dock division of Belfast, McManus, Curry, Farrell, McCann and others.

John McKeague, a shopkeeper, emerged as a more-militant-than-Paisley Protestant, and he was joined by a group of men who kept their identities out of the fracas. Between them these men formed the Ulster Volunteer Force, branded illegal like the IRA but never as often in the field as their Catholic counterparts.

Government leaders came and when they seemed to be wavering towards the granting of civil rights they, too, went. O'Neill, the most genuine of all, Chichester-Clarke, never more than a compromise, and Faulkner who always looked like being the last of the line.

These were the people in the middle of what was never more than a tragic little war; as tragic a war as the Irish ever fought in. But then this sort of conflict – Irishman fighting Irishman and in the background the spectre of religion – could never be anything else. In it there was seldom such a thing as military strategy – after all there wasn't likely to be, the whole affair had muddled along under the blanket title of 'the Irish trouble' for so long that everyone thought it could never rate as anything more than this. The same Irish question had brought risings and wars in 1155, 1172, 1210, 1227, 1231, 1315, 1534, 1641, 1661, 1688, 1710, 1798, 1803, and so on into the twentieth century. In fact, the Irish situation was very much a British situation and, as such, had for the British a bewildering air about it. A British soldier could see himself in some far-flung corner of the Empire fighting an Arab or a Turk or a Cypriot. At least he had the chance of recognising them and sorting out his enemies from his friends simply by looks, but in the North of Ireland the people he was supposed to be fighting looked the same as those he was supposed to be protecting. This bewilderment was expressed by one British officer who looked at a group of old women facing him and said: 'They are our enemies . . . what can you do?'

It was a bewildering situation for everyone. One terrorist was a hero in one camp, one hero was a murderer in another; terrorist, guerrilla, hero, murderer, it all depended on which side of the fence you were on.

Take the man who through many a week fought singlehanded against the British army. His ploy was to stand on a corner unconcerned with all that was going on around him, no matter what it was. His target was the scout cars which roved through Belfast. When one approached, the man slid around the corner and waited. When the unsuspecting army car drove up, the man leapt with all the agility of a super athlete on to the car and fired a shot through the aperture. It was the work of a hero if you were on one side and the work of a madman if you were on the other. After five or six such sorties in which he is supposed to have injured a number of soldiers, the man inevitably fell into a trap. A scout car rounded a corner slowly but was tailed so tightly by another that the man was a fair target as soon as he moved. But again his speed proved too much even for guns; despite being hit twice he still managed a getaway through the burrow-like streets of Belfast.

'The troubles' – the British were using this euphemism again – went on with incidents like this taking every day and shaking it into a nightmare. Everyone was jumpy; local shops and offices became the targets of roving bombers; the giant superstores of which Belfast was so proud were being hit continually. Roof scuttling, bomb throwing, catcalling, snipers, shouting mobs – each in turn escalated the situation. A car backfiring even brought death as soldiers, always on edge, immediately fired on it.

Like everything about the Northern Ireland situation, one incident rested on another and that on another, pyramid style. Go back to the first time a soldier shot at a backfiring car . . . the soldier honestly believed he was being shot at. A test afterwards by the army proved that the man was driving a van liable to backfire.

It seemed a simple, if unfortunate, situation to the army. Jerky and nervy under continual strain they were not prepared, like any man, to take chances when their own lives were in danger.

But on this morning a man died; to the local Catholic population another martyr has been added to the growing litany. Dignified and determined they gather on the spot. Soon it is only the women who are left; they sit on the roadside, then they kneel and pray for the dead man. They decide that a day's vigil will be held for him and that no lorry or car will pass that spot again until the sun has set. When a car approaches they wave a black flag and send the vehicle down a side street, away from their place of mourning.

When tensions are like this, people, even the most hard-headed, decide to co-operate, but one car approaches and the driver decides that nothing will divert him from his way. There's a man, a woman and two children in the car. The man defies the women to stop him. Sticks and stones are thrown by the now jeering women as the man edges his car through the group. He escapes into the open road, but not for long. Ahead of him he suddenly sees a crowd just breaking off from a running battle with soldiers. They have decided to upend all traffic; the speeding car is now their target. The terrible situation no doubt dawns on the driver and his family. He can't help but slow the car down as the big crowd blocks the road. Kicking, bashing and rocking the car the crowd take no notice of the terrified occupants. The driver sees a gap in the crowd, he accelerates for it. At that moment a fourteen-year-old boy steps out and is cascaded into the road by the rushing car. He is left on the road, almost dead. The driver dare not stop.

Even yet the trouble is not over. Another car speeds after the hit-and-run driver. When the confrontation comes the now utterly shattered driver is pulled from the car and beaten solidly in front of his own family. He lives. So does the boy. And no action will be taken. It is an insignificant incident; just part of one day in a war where no one escaped, where no one can dream of peace again, where even the dying must be left alone unless you want to throw your life in the open. Even a priest, going to adminster to a dying man, is shot down and dies.

Now and again the IRA showed its own brand of audacity that had one South American writer describing them as being 'either the coolest guerrillas in the world – or the stupidest'. However, there seemed little that was stupid about the raid they carried out on a Belfast hospital to rescue one of their injured comrades. Gerald Fitzgerald had been captured after an ambush. He was shot twice and eventually taken to Belfast's Royal Victoria Hospital where he was operated on for the removal of a bullet in his thigh. Lying in bed, dazed after the operation, he wondered what was going to happen to him. So too did his IRA comrades and they devised a plan to rescue Fitzgerald.

Five men arrived at the hospital dressed in white overalls and filtered through the wards singly to meet outside their comrade's ward. 'I was lying there,' said Fitzgerald afterwards, 'when I saw this man coming through the door . . . he was armed with a revolver. He told me to come with him. I got out of bed, he gave me an arm to lean on and we walked out of the hospital . . . I was dressed only in a hospital gown.'

Fitzgerald was driven away, but only to a house a few hundred yards from the hospital where he was safely installed before the hunt for him got under way. He stayed in the house a few days but his companions decided he wanted more expert medical aid than they could manage, so they put him in a car and drove for the Irish border. But just as they were approaching the border crossing spot they saw an army checkpoint.

Again luck was on their side. There was a small shop just before the checkpoint. They stopped the car and went in and bought ice-pops. Then they sat on the side of the roadway eating them and waved to the soldiers.

'The soldiers waved back,' said Fitzgerald, 'but in an hour's time they had decided to call it a day and drove away.' Unhampered, the group crossed the border where the wounded man was treated. A few months afterwards he came out in the open again 'to deny rumours that I'm dead,' he joked.

Most of the badly injured IRA men were taken to hospitals in the Republic of Ireland. Now and again they met with unforeseen obstacles, mainly checkpoints set up by either the Royal Ulster Constabulary, the Ulster Defence Regiment or the army. One story tells of a man who was driven around the border area for two days before they could find an unmanned crossing point. He kept one arm tucked into his pocket . . . his hand had been blown off in an explosion.

Bombs were the main armament of war used as the situation escalated. In the first months of the war there were few bombs but two years later they became a thrice daily hazard. In fact 1969 saw only nineteen explosions but in the first ten months of 1971 there were seven hundred and fifty – not counting the army's tally of four hundred bombs dealt with before they exploded. The amounts of explosives used were huge – some even taking 25lb of explosive, enough to wreck a large building. 'You can always tell an IRA bomb,' a British army expert said, 'by the amount of explosive . . . they are very generous in their use of gelignite.'

The most common bomb of all was the petrol bomb. On one occasion in Derry these were made openly in one of the massive confrontations that city has witnessed during the years. A petrol tanker was hijacked in one street and a returning milk lorry in another. Brought together they formed the main ingredients for an almost endless supply of bombs. It wasn't long before the tanker had been christened in large white letters 'Free Ireland Bomb Factory'. But, as well as the petrol bomb, nail bombs were frequent – indeed anything in a Coke tin, a salt tin, a cigarette packet, even a contraceptive, was likely to maim.

Bombs became so numerous they could even prompt cartoons in Northern papers. One showed two men meeting in the street both carrying bulky parcels. 'Tell me,' says one, 'what time is it by your bomb, Jimmy?'

The arms used in the fight were not, of course, restricted to bombs. It has been said that if it was made to hurt, maim, gas or kill, it has been used in this conflict – by one side or the other. Certainly the British Army had the most modern methods of warfare available; the militant Protestants had a great wealth of firepower – especially in the legally organised gun clubs throughout the area; the IRA had a diverse collection of everything from pellet guns through Bren guns to rocket launchers. Documented evidence shows that among the weapons used by the IRA was a German Mauser over eighty years old; US Springfield rifles; German 7.92 mm Gewehr rifles and even the fantastically firepowered .50 Browning belt fan machine gun.

It is claimed that the backbone of the IRA firepower has been provided by ex-US army gunware – the .300 M1 carbine, the fully automatic M2 and the later version of the same gun, commonly known as the 'grease gun'. The rattle of a Thompson gun still echoes in Belfast – it has a place in the hearts of most Republicans having seen service in many a scrimmage since its manufacture in the 1920s.

The IRA arsenal has been built up through many long years and from occasional injections of new weapons through sources in both Europe and America. The arms find, late in 1971, on the quayside at Cobh in County Cork gave a valuable clue as to how many of the arms were brought in. A trunk containing sub-machine guns and hand grenades had travelled from America in the baggage hold of the *QE2*. Most of the luggage had been cleared through Customs but some cases remained; when Customs men investigated they found a whole array of new weapons and ammunition. It was one catch . . . but everyone wondered just how often the same ruse had been successful.

So the war in Northern Ireland went on . . . the constant attacks, the bombings and the killings and then someone believed they had found an answer. Internment was introduced. A quick sweep and, the world was told, now the whole thing was over: the main antagonists were behind barbed wire. But it was merely another fuse to the whole affair. Whereas sixty people had died in almost two years, in the three months after internment the figure had risen to over a hundred and forty. And more tragedy was added – terror now tunnelled through the whole population. The knock on the door after midnight became the first frightening suggestion that some member of a family was being 'lifted'. The dread thought of brain-washing and torture only brought on more frightening killings, shootings and bombings and opened the chasm of bewilderment wider.

Where would it all end . . . and when?

An old man provided the answer to a soldier. He was going home one evening and he was chatting to the soldier.

'Are you worried,' he asked the young Yorkshireman.

'I am,' came the reply, 'and wouldn't you be too?'

'I would,' said the old man, looking carefully into the fading light, 'because I know when it will all end.'

'You do?' enthused the soldier. 'Really end? When?'

The old man began to walk away. 'In a thousand bloody years,' he said quietly.

PART 6

Some Fighting Irish Songs

Some Fighting Irish Songs

The Fighting Race

by Joseph I C Clarke

'Read out the names!' and Burke sat back
And Kelly drooped his head,
While Shea – they call him Scholar Jack –
Went down the list of dead.
Officers, seamen, gunners, marines,
The crews of the gig and yawl,
The bearded man and the lad in his teens
Carpenters, coal passers – all.
Then knocking the ashes from out of his pipe,
Said Burke in an offhand way:
'We're all in that dead man's list, by Cripe!
Kelly and Burke and Shea.'
'Well, here's to the Maine, and I'm sorry for Spain,'
Said Kelly and Burke and Shea.

'Wherever there's Kellys there's trouble,' said Burke.
'Wherever fighting's the game,
Or a spice of danger in grown man's work,'
Said Kelly, 'you'll find my name.'
'And do we fall short,' said Burke, getting mad,
'When it's touch and go for life?'
Said Shea, 'It's thirty-odd years, bedad,
Since I charged to drum and fife
Up Marye's Heights, and my old canteen
Stopped a rebel ball on its way.
There were blossoms of blood on our sprigs of green –
Kelly and Burke and Shea
And the dead didn't brag.' 'Well, here's to the flag!'
Said Kelly, Burke and Shea.

'I wish't was in Ireland, for there's the place,'
 Said Burke, 'that we'd die by right,
In the cradle of our soldier race,
 After one good stand-up fight.
My grandfather fell on Vinegar Hill
 And fighting was not his trade;
But the rusty pike's in the cabin still
 With Hessian blood on the blade.'
'Aye, aye,' said Kelly, 'the pikes were great
 When the word was "clear the way!"
We were thick on the roll in Ninety-eight –
 Kelly and Burke and Shea.'
'Well here's to the pike and the sword and the like!'
 Said Kelly and Burke and Shea.

And Shea, the scholar, with rising joy,
 Said, 'We were at Ramillies;
We left our bones at Fontenoy
 And up in the Pyrenees.
Before Dunkirk, on Landen's plain,
 Cremona, Lille and Ghent,
We're all over Austria, France and Spain,
 Wherever they pitched a tent
We've died for England from Waterloo
 To Egypt and Dargai;
And there's still enough for a corps or a crew,
 Kelly and Burke and Shea.'
'Well, here's to good honest fighting blood!'
 Said Kelly and Burke and Shea.

'Oh the fighting races don't die out,
    If they seldom die in bed,
For love is first in their hearts, no doubt,'
    Said Burke; then Kelly said:
'When Michael, the Irish Archangel, stands,
    The angel with the sword,
And the battle dead from a hundred lands
    Are ranged in one big hoard
Our line, that for Gabriel's trumpet waits,
    Will stretch three deep that day,
From Jehoshaphat to the Golden Gates –
    Kelly and Burke and Shea.'
'Well, here's thank God for the race and the sod!'
    Said Kelly and Burke and Shea.

O'Donnell Abu

by Michael Joseph McCann

Proudly the note of the trumpet is sounding,
Loudly the war cries arise on the gale;
Fleetly the steed by Lough Swilly is bounding,
To join the thick squadrons in Saimear's green vale.
    On, every mountaineer
    Strangers to flight and fear!
Rush to the standard of dauntless Red Hugh!
    Bonnaught and gallowglass,
    Throng from each mountain pass;
On for old Erin, 'O'Donnell Abu!'

Princely O'Neill to our aid is advancing
With many a chieftain and warrior clan
A thousand proud steeds in his vanguard are prancing
'Neath the borderers brave from the banks of the Bann;
    Many a heart shall quail
    Under its coat of mail;
Deeply the merciless foeman shall rue,
    When on his ear shall ring
    Borne on the breezes' wing,
Tir Connell's dread war-cry 'O'Donnell Abu!'

Sacred the cause of Clan Connaill's defending,
The altars we kneel at, the homes of our sires;
Ruthless the ruin the foe is extending
Midnight is red with the plunderers' fires.
    On with O'Donnell then
    Fight the old fight again,
Sons of Tir Connell, all valiant and true.
    Make the false Saxon feel,
    Erin's avenging steel!
Strike for your country 'O'Donnell Abu!'

The Rising of the Moon

by John Keegan Casey

Tell me, tell me Sean O'Farrell, tell me why you hurry so,
Hush, a buchaill hush and listen, and his cheeks were all aglow,
I bear orders from the Captain, get you ready quick and soon,
For the pikes must be together by the rising of the moon.

'O! Then tell me, Sean O'Farrell, where the gathering is to be?'
'In the old spot by the river, right well known to you and me.
One word more, for signal token whistle up the marchin' tune,
With your pike upon your shoulder at the rising of the moon.'

Out from many a mud wall cabin eyes were watchin' through the night.
Many a manly heart was throbbing for that blessed warning light;
Murmurs passed along the valley, like the banshee's lonesome croon,
And a thousand blades were flashing at the rising of the moon.

There beside the singing river that dark mass of men was seen,
High above their shining weapons flew their own beloved green,
'Death to every foe and traitor! forward! strike the marchin' tune!
And hurra! my boys, for freedom; 'tis the rising of the moon!'

Well they fought for poor old Ireland, and full bitter was their fate;
Oh! what glorious pride and sorrow fill the name of Ninety-eight.
But, thank God, there still are beating strong young hearts in manhood's bloom,
Who will follow in their footsteps at the rising of the moon.

High Germany

Chorus:
All for thee love, all for thee love,
The rout has now begun.
And I must go a marching to the beating of the drum.
Come dress yourself in all your best
And come along with me
I'll take you to the wars m'love in High Germany.

I'll buy for you a horse my love
And on it you will ride
And all of my delight will be in riding be your side.
We'll stop at every alehouse
And drink when we are dry
We'll be true to one another and get married by and by.

Chorus:

O cursed be those cruel wars
That ever did they rise
And out of merrie England pass many a man likewise.
They took my true love from me
Likewise my brothers three
And sent them to the wars m'love in High Germany.

Chorus:

My friends I do not value
And my foes I do not fear
For now my fine love's left me and wanders far and near
But when my baby it is born
And smiling on my knee
I'll think of handsome Willie in High Germany.

Chorus:

Captain Fowler

Come, all you croppies, where'er you dwell,
Good news for you I have to tell,
Of an orangeman who was sent to hell,
And they called him Captain Fowler.

When Dick Fowler at the gates arrived,
He found that they were opened wide;
Good morrow, good morrow, the devils cried,
And surrounded him with blazes.

They threw him into a fiery den,
Among his brother-orangemen,
Stay there, my boy, and roast your shins
On the hot flags of damnation.

A fiery cap on his head they placed,
A blazing sash all round his waist,
Two bloody bells on his shoulders each,
Then he looked like a warlike soldier.

Says Fowler, now, if a croppy come
With a drop of water to cool my tongue,
I'd own to him I've done great wrong,
In hopes he would relieve me.

Says Belzebub, how can you tell
That ever a croppy was sent to hell?
It was for Freedom these boys fell,
And heaven is their station.

The Boyne Water

July the first, of a morning clear,
one thousand six hundred and ninety,
King William did his men prepare,
of thousands he had thirty,
King James he pitched his tents between
the lines for to retire
But King William threw his bomb balls
and set them all on fire.

King William called his officers,
saying: 'Gentlemen, mind your station,
And let your valour here be shown
before this Irish nation;
My brazen walls let no man break,
and your subtle foes you'll scatter,
Be sure you show them good English play
as you go over the water.'

Both foot and horse they marched on,
intending them to batter,
But brave Duke Schomberg he was shot
as he crossed over the water,
When the King William did observe
the brave Duke Schomberg falling,
He reined his horse with a heavy heart,
on the Enniskilleners calling:

'What will you do for me, brave boys –
see yonder men retreating?
Our enemies encouraged are
and English drums are beating':
He says, 'my boys, feel no dismay
at the losing of one commander
For God shall be our King this day
and I'll be general under.'

Within four yards of our fore front,
    before a shot was fired,
A sudden snuff they got that day,
    which little they desired;
For horse and man fell to the ground,
    and some hung in their saddle;
Others turned up their forked ends,
    which we call coup de ladle.

Prince Eugene's regiment was the next,
    on our right hand advanced,
Into a field of standing wheat,
    where Irish horses pranced –
But the brandy ran so in their heads,
    their senses all did scatter,
They little thought to leave their bones
    that day at the Boyne Water.

Both men and horse lay on the ground,
    and many there lay bleeding,
I saw no sickles there that day –
    but, sure, there was sharp shearing;
And in the dead time of the night,
    they set the fields on fire,
And long before the morning light
    to Dublin they did retire.

Now, praise God, all true Protestants,
    and heaven's and earth's Creator,
For the deliverance that he sent
    our enemies to scatter.
The Church his foes will pine away,
    like churlish-hearted Nabal,
For our deliverer came this day
    like the great Zorobabel.

So praise God, all true Protestants
and I will say no further,
But had the Papists gained the day,
there would have been open murder.
Although King James and many more
were ne'er that way inclined,
It was not in their power to stop
what the rabble they designed.

Awful Battle at Vicksburg

You feeling-hearted Irishmen and maidens, now draw near,
It's when that you peruse these lines you can't but shed a tear,
When you think on our misery 'twill cause your hearts full sore,
When I relate the hardships all on Columbia's shore.

It's since this cruel war began, most grievous for to say,
Alas employment has declined and commerce did decay,
Has caused our Irish boys to list for the battle-field array,
To fight our own relations here, all in America.

The South prepared for action upon the battle ground,
Our cavalry and infantry with cannons planted round,
The Stars and Stripes does proudly float unwantin' the contest,
Old Erin's flag on both sides hoisted by Irish hearts arrest.

Like thunderbolts the balls do fly from the artillery,
The fire and smoke ascend the sky most dismal for to see,
The brother fights the brother and the father fights the son,
And after all no sign at all of this sad war being done.

Thro' fields of blood we have waded, where cannon balls do roar,
And many a brave commander lay bleeding in his gore,
And heaps of Irish heroes brave on the plains there lay,
That were both killed and wounded there all in America.

It would melt your hearts with pity for to see the soldiers' wives
Looking for their dead husbands with sad and dismal cries,
The children crying Mama, sure we may rue the day
We lost our own poor dadas all in America.

After each and every battle, see the memory of the dead,
Some wanting legs and arms, and more without their heads,
In pits some thousands here do lie far from their native clay,
To take a long and silent sleep until the Judgment Day.

Many an Irish mother to the Post Office ran,
In hopes a welcome letter should return from her son,
Alas but little do they know they fell in crimson gore,
Their bones lie mouldering with the dust all on Columbia's shore.

America, once happy land, but now a scene of woe,
President Lincoln hates the bloody South, and their slavery also,
For thousands of our Irish boys without employment strong,
The widows and their orphans dear, all in America.

Good Christians all! now bear in mind and mark the words I say,
When you are at devotion, let it be night or day,
Then for these Irish soldiers brave you earnestly will pray;
For those poor souls in battle fell all in America.

Johnny, I Hardly Knew ye

While going the road to sweet Athy,
    Hurroo! hurroo!
While going the road to sweet Athy,
    Hurroo! hurroo!
While going the road to sweet Athy,
A stick in my hand and a drop in my eye,
A doleful damsel I heard cry:
    'Och Johnny, I hardly knew ye!
    With drums and guns, and guns and drums
    The enemy nearly slew ye;
My darling dear, you look so queer,
Och, Johnny, I hardly knew ye!

'Where are your eyes that looked so mild?
    Hurroo! hurroo!
Where are your eyes that looked so mild?
    Hurroo! hurroo!
Where are your eyes that looked so mild?
When my poor heart you first beguiled,
Why did you run from me and the child?
    Och Johnny, I hardly knew ye!
    With drums, etc.

'Where are the legs with which you run?
    Hurroo! hurroo!
Where are the legs with which you run?
    Hurroo! hurroo!
Where are the legs with which you run?
When you went to carry a gun,
Indeed, your dancing days are done!
    Och, Johnny, I hardly knew ye!
    With drums, etc.

'It grieved my heart to see you sail,
    Hurroo! hurroo!
It grieved my heart to see you sail,
    Hurroo! hurroo!
It grieved my heart to see you sail,
Though from my heart you took beg-bail;
Like a cod you're doubled up head and tail.
    Och, Johnny, I hardly knew ye!
    With drums, etc.

'You haven't an arm and you haven't a leg,
    Hurroo! hurroo!
You haven't an arm and you haven't a leg,
    Hurroo! hurroo!
You haven't an arm and you haven't a leg,
You're an eyeless, noseless, chickenless egg;
You'll have to be put with a bowl to beg.
    Och, Johnny, I hardly knew ye!
    With drums, etc.

'I'm happy for to see you home,
    Hurroo! hurroo!
I'm happy for to see you home,
    Hurroo! hurroo!
I'm happy for to see you home,
All from the island of Sulloon,
So low in flesh, so high in bone;
    Och, Johnny, I hardly knew ye!
    With drums, etc.

'But sad as it is to see you so,
    Hurroo! hurroo!
But sad as it is to see you so,
    Hurroo! hurroo!
But sad as it is to see you so,
And to think of you now as an object of woe,
Your Peggy'll still keep ye on as her beau;
    Och, Johnny, I hardly knew ye!
    With drums and guns, and guns and drums
    The enemy nearly slew ye;
My darling dear, you look so queer,
Och, Johnny, I hardly knew ye!'

The Burial of Sir John Moore

by Charles Wolfe

Not a drum was heard, not a funeral note,
As his corse to the rampart we hurried;
Not a soldier discharged his farewell shot
O'er the grave where our hero we buried.

We buried him darkly at dead of night,
The sods with our bayonets turning,
By the struggling moonbeam's misty light,
And the lantern dimly burning.

No useless coffin enclosed his breast,
Not in sheet or in shroud we wound him;
But he lay like a warrior taking his rest,
With his martial cloak around him.

Few and short were the prayers we said,
And we spoke not a word of sorrow;
But we steadfastly gazed on the face that was dead,
And we bitterly thought of the morrow.

We thought, as we hollowed his narrow bed,
And smoothed down his lonely pillow,
That the foe and the stranger would tread o'er his head,
And we far away on the billow!

Lightly they'll talk of the spirit that's gone,
And o'er his cold ashes upbraid him, –
But little he'll reck, if they let him sleep on
In the grave where a Briton has laid him.

But half of our heavy task was done,
When the clock struck the hour for retiring;
And we heard the distant and random gun
That the foe was sullenly firing.

Slowly and sadly we laid him down,
From the field of his fame, fresh and gory;
We carved not a line, and we raised not a stone –
But we left him alone with his glory!

Boulavogue

At Boulavogue, as the sun was setting
O'er the green May meadows of Shelmalier,
A rebel band set the heather blazing,
And brought the neighbours from far and near.
Then Father Murphy, of old Kilcormack,
Spurred up the rocks with a warning cry –
Arm! Arm! he cried, for I've come to lead you –
Now priest and people must fight or die!

He led us on 'gainst the coming soldiers,
And the cowardly Yeomen we put to flight;
Down at the Harrow, the Boys of Wexford
Showed Bookey's regiment how men could fight!
Look out for hirelings, King George of England,
Search every kingdom that breeds a slave!
For Father Murphy, of the County Wexford,
Sweeps o'er the earth like a mighty wave!

We took Camolin and Enniscorthy,
And Wexford storming, drove out our foes;
'Twas at Slieve Kiltha our pikes were reeking
With the crimson stream of the beaten Yeos.
At Tubberneering and Ballyellis
Full many a Hessian lay in his gore!
Ah, Father Murphy, had aid come over,
A green flag floated from shore to shore!

At Vinegar Hill, o'er the pleasant Slaney,
Our heroes vainly stood back to back,
And the Yeos at Tullow took Father Murphy,
And burned his body upon the rack.
God give you glory, brave Father Murphy,
And open heaven to all your men;
The cause that called you may call to-morrow
In another war for the Green again.

The Inniskilling Dragoon

A beautiful maiden of fame and renown,
A gentleman's daughter from Monaghan town,
As she drove by the barracks this beautiful maid
Stood up in her coach to see the Dragoons on parade.

They were all dressed up the like of gentlemen's sons
With their bright shining sabres and their carbine guns,
Their brass mounted pistols she noted them too
All because she loved an Inniskilling Dragoon.

Chorus:
Fare thee well Inniskilling, fare thee well for awhile,
On all your fair waters and every green isle
And when the war is over, we'll return in full bloom
And ye'll all welcome home the Inniskilling Dragoons.

O Flora, dear Flora, your good pardon I crave,
For its now and forever, dear, that I am your slave
Your parents have slighted me morn, night and noon
All because that you loved an Inniskilling Dragoon.

O William, dear William, don't heed what they say,
For children their parents should always obey.
But when you leave Ireland they will all change their tune,
Saying, the God go with you Inniskilling Dragoon.

Chorus:
Fare thee well, Inniskilling, fare thee well for awhile
On all your fair waters and every green isle
And when the war is over, we'll return in full bloom
The sixth loyal, Royal Inniskilling Dragoons.

The Brave Tipperary Boy

Draw near, you sons of Granuaile, attend unto my song,
I'll sing for you a verse or two – I'll not detain you long;
'Tis of a valiant Irishman, his praises I will sing,
For £10,000 on the first of June he has now challenged King.

'Tis true I am an Irishman from the town of Templemore,
And many a better man than King I left all in his gore;
'Tis not for money I'm going to fight, it's plainly to be seen,
But for old Ireland's credit and the dear old shamrock green.

John Morrissey is my name – my age is forty-three;
Some people say I am too old to gain the victory,
But on the first of November, when I stand in the ring,
I'm sure I will play Patrick's Day upon the ribs of King.

When I was joined in wedlock bands, the truth I will relate,
A promise to my wedded wife I was obliged to make:
That fighting for the future I certainly would shun,
But I must have satisfaction for what John Heenan done.

The first man that I ever fought, it was the Buffalo Boy,
The Yankees all were sure that day my life he would destroy;
But John gained the victory and that without much noise,
I played for him that favourite tune, The Brave Tipperary Boys.

Then Sam the Black he was the next I own I did subdue,
The Russian Sailor and Shepherd I half killed 'tis true;
I never feared an Englishman or Yankee in the Ring,
But I tell you true I will subdue the English bully, King.

'Tis nor for the sake of money nor any other wealth,
Nor neither is it for the sake of the English Belt,
But for the honour of old Ireland, as you may plainly see,
I'll fight or die all in the Ring or gain the victory.

Now to conclude these verses, I have no more to say,
That courage may not fail him and may he gain the day;
Come fill the glasses to the top until they do flow o'er,
And toast to gallant Morrisey, the pride of Erin's shore.

The Kelly Gang

Oh, there's not a dodge worth knowing
Or showing, that's going,
But you'll learn (this isn't blowing)
From the bold Kelly Gang.

We have mates where'er we go
That somehow let us know
The approach of every foe
To the bold Kelly Gang.

There's not a peeler riding
Wombat ranges, hill or siding
But would rather be for hiding
Though he'd like to see us hang.

We thin their ranks
We rob the banks
And say no thanks
For what we do –
Oh the terror of the Camp is the bold Kelly Gang.

Then if you want a spree
Come with me and you'll see
How grand it is to be
In the bold Kelly Gang.

Bold Jack Donahoe

'Twas of a valiant highwayman and outlaw of disdain,
Who'd scorn to live in slavery or wear a convict's chain;
His name it was John Donahoe of courage and renown –
He'd scorn to live in slavery or humble to the Crown.

This bold undaunted highwayman, as you may understand,
Was banished for his natural life from Erin's happy land.
In Dublin City of renown, where his first breath he drew,
It's there they titled him the brave and bold Jack Donahoe.

He scarce had been a twelve-month on the Australian shore,
When he took to the highway, as oft he had before.
Brave Macnamara, Underwood, Webber and Walmsley too,
These were the four associates of bold Jack Donahoe.

As Jack and his companions roved out one afternoon,
Not thinking that the pains of death would overcome so soon,
To their surprise five horse police appeared all in their view,
And in quick time they did advance to take Jack Donahoe.

'Come, come, you cowardly rascals, oh, do not run away!
We'll fight them man to man, my boys, their number's only
three;
For I'd rather range the bush around, like dingo or kangaroo,
Than work one hour for Government,' said bold Jack Donahoe.

'Oh, no,' said cowardly Walmsley, 'to that I won't agree;
I see they're still adavncing us – their number's more than three.
And if we wait we'll be too late, the battle we will rue.'
'Then begone from me, you cowardly dog,' replied Jack
Donahoe.

The Sergeant of the horse police discharged his car-a-bine,
And called aloud to Donahoe 'Will you fight or resign?'
'Resign, no, no! I never will, unto your cowardly crew,
For to-day I'll fight with all my might,' cried bold Jack
  Donahoe.

The Sergeant then, in a hurry his party to divide,
Placed one to fire in front of him, and another on each side;
The Sergeant and the Corporal, they both fired too,
Till the fatal ball had pierced the heart of bold Jack Donahoe.

Six rounds he fought those horse police before the fatal ball,
Which pierced his heart with cruel smart, caused Donahoe to
  fall;
And as he closed his mournful eyes he bade this world adieu,
Saying 'Good people all, pray for the soul of poor Jack
  Donahoe.'

There were Freincy, Grant, bold Robin Hood, Brennan and
  O'Hare;
With Donahoe this highwayman none of them could compare.
But now he's gone to Heaven I hope, with saints and angels too–
May the Lord have mercy on the soul of brave Jack Donahoe.

The Rebel

by Padraic Pearse

I am come of the seed of the people, the people that sorrow,
That have no treasure but hope,
No riches laid up but a memory
Of an ancient glory.
My mother bore me in bondage, in bondage my mother was
  born,
I am the blood of serfs;

The children with whom I have played, the men and women with whom I have eaten,
Have had masters over them, they have been under the lash of masters,
And though gentle, have served churls;
The hands that have touched mine, the dear hands whose touch is familiar to me,
Have worn shameful manacles, have been bitten at the wrist by manacles,
Have grown hard with the manacles and the task-work of strangers,
I am flesh of the flesh of these lowly, I am bone of their bone,
I that have never submitted;
I that have a soul greater than the souls of my people's masters,
I that have vision and prophecy and the gift of fiery speech,
I that have spoken with God on the top of His holy hill.
And because I am of the people, I understand the people,
I am sorrowful with their sorrow, I am hungry with their desire:
My heart has been heavy with the grief of mothers,
My eyes have been wet with the tears of children,
I have yearned with old wistful men,
And laughed or cursed with young men;
Their shame is my shame, and I have reddened for it,
Reddened for that they have gone in want, while others have been full,
Reddened for that they have walked in fear of lawyers and of their jailors
With their writs of summons and their handcuffs,
Men mean and cruel!
I could have borne stripes on my body rather than this shame of my people.
And now I speak, being full of vision;

I speak to my people, and I speak in my people's name to the
masters of my people.
I say to my people that they are holy, that they are august,
despite their chains,
That they are greater than those that hold them, and stronger
and purer,
That they have but need of courage, and to call on the name of
their God,
God the unforgetting, the dear God that loves the peoples
For whom He died naked, suffering shame.
And I say to my people's masters: Beware,
Beware of the thing that is coming, beware of the risen people,
Who shall take what ye would not give. Did ye think to
conquer the people,
Or that Law is stronger than life and than men's desire to be
free?
We will try it out with you, ye that have harried and held,
Ye that have bullied and bribed, tyrants, hypocrites!

Index

C

D

I

P

Q